OUR MODERN BLENDED FAMILY

D1446162

OUR MODERN
BLENDED
FAMILY

A Practical Guide
to Creating a Happy Home

Danielle Schlagel

**ROCKRIDGE
PRESS**

For general information on our other products and services or to obtain technical support, please contact our Customer Care Department within the U.S. at (866) 744-2665, or outside the U.S. at (510) 253-0500.

Rockridge Press publishes its books in a variety of electronic and print formats. Some content that appears in print may not be available in electronic books, and vice versa.

Interior and Cover Designer: Sean Doyle
Art Producer: Hillary Frileck
Editor: Eliza Kirby
Production Editor: Ashley Polikoff
Cover and interior illustrations used under license from iStock.com

ISBN: Print 978-1-64152-856-6 | eBook 978-1-64152-857-3
R0

For the blended family that raised me.
For the blended family I raise.
For those who love others' children.
For those who love mine.

CONTENTS

INTRODUCTION

Life has a way of giving what you need, but doesn't always pan out as originally imagined. Most people don't grow up longing for divorce proceedings or wishing to be a stepparent. Life unfolds as it does, and making the necessary adjustments can be challenging as you move past what you once envisioned for yourself. You may find, though, a new life that's filled with love, laughter, and happiness—maybe more than you first thought possible.

You see, when I was six years old, my parents divorced. I have one full sibling, two half-siblings, and three stepsiblings. You may be picturing a tumultuous childhood filled with arguments, grief, and bitterness. That would be an understandable assumption, but an incorrect one. My parents divorced with grace. They continued to work together for several more decades, alongside my now stepfather. My stepmother comes to events at my mother's home, and my daughter loves all four of my parents completely.

Not only am I a child of divorce, but I am also a licensed professional counselor, licensed addictions counselor, and registered play therapist-supervisor. I have done this work—specializing with children, parents, and families—for more than a decade. I've devoted my life to helping families see one another with greater, more compassionate clarity. Much of my work has been in helping parents through the most challenging parenting situations, like trauma, divorce, and blending families. I have been honored to be a part of all this.

Suffice it to say, I know how to blend families. You would think that when the opportunity arose in my own life, I'd have found blending my own family to be a breeze, right? But when I met my husband, I had no idea what was in store for us. His daughter had just turned three, and I was living out of state. We fell in love easily, and I was so excited to be a part of this ready-made life. Six years have passed now, our older girl (who for simplicity's sake, I'll refer to as my stepdaughter) is a rising fourth grader, and our younger daughter (who I'll refer to as my daughter) is almost three years old. I, too, am living in the thick of blended family life. If I'm being honest, and I will be throughout this book, I'll tell you we've made mistakes. Our road hasn't been an easy one, and I don't write before you as some mystical stepmom goddess who did everything perfectly. Trust me, I did not. Blending families is hard work.

But what are blended families? They come in all shapes and sizes. You're a blended family because one or both of you have children from a previous relationship, and you have chosen to become a family. You may have once been married but are no longer because of divorce or loss, you may have never been married but still co-parent, or you may be a single parent bringing in new family members. Perhaps you're just starting to come together as a blended family. Maybe you've been at this for a while and are still struggling or in need of a refresher. Wherever you stand today, you're up for a tough job—though a worth-while one.

Being a parent can be a difficult job all on its own. It comes with long nights, short days, and endless to-dos. It includes the worry, care, and time you put into your children. When you add blending a family into the mix, everything gets more complicated. You may have many questions. How will we come together? What will happen to our relationship? How will we co-parent? What will our future bring?

Blended families travel different roads than other families. Sure, this road will have bumps, sharp curves, and sometimes drastic changes in altitude. But you know what? All of these experiences make you stronger. I'm here to say that having a happy blended family is possible. I'm here to say you can do this. You can laugh with your children, nourish your partnership, navigate tricky waters, and come out the other side with love and ease. Some of our most beautiful and satisfying experiences in life come as the result of a little extra elbow grease.

Having a blended family can bring such joy. There are moments my family shares that fill my heart with gratitude. Sometimes that's listening to the laughter between our girls, hearing the chatter when all 18 of us from my mom's side get together, seeing the excitement and joy on my daughter's face when she gets to visit with either of my parents and their partners, my daughter cheering for my half-sister at recitals, and those sweet moments when my stepdaughter emulates something I do in my daily routine. Thinking back to moments like these reminds me that the potential for love is endless.

This book starts out with an overview of blended families. We walk through how to define your family and partnership, and set healthy goals. We discuss how to prioritize your children, process difficult feelings, and settle into your new home. Chapter 2 deals in more depth with ways to put extra care into what is bringing your family together: your relationship. This will include some information about co-parenting. We get more into parenting, though, in chapter 3, in understanding boundaries, limits, and discipline. We look at how each partner parents and ways you can parent better together. Chapters 4 and 5 bring us through daily life and how best to integrate extended family, including bringing in a new baby and navigating relationships with adult children. We end our journey together focusing on your bright future as a family.

Throughout this book I use language that's meant to speak to as many as possible. When I say *children* and *kids*, for example, you may have only one child or your "children" may be grown. When I refer to *biological parents*, I am including those of you who have adopted. With the understanding that you may not have been previously married and may or may not be currently, I will refer to your current relationship as your *partner*, and any previous relationship as *ex-spouse*, including those you may have lost. The use of these terms is to help differentiate. The overarching point, though, is to help you navigate the creation of a family through a working partnership in your current relationship.

As inclusive as I've tried to be, however, I may have missed a spot. If you find that a particular point of the book doesn't apply, either skip it or look for the underlying meaning. Most often, the overall message will be to enter your new family with care, communication, and hope. While remaining neutral, I present the realities of blending families, with the myriad challenges and joys. Because blended families occur in all backgrounds, religions, and cultures, everyone can benefit from the information presented here. This book is for modern blended families.

CHAPTER ONE
A New Family

Welcome to your journey. You're here because you've decided to bring a new family together. Your family makeup will be uniquely yours, but the path you're on is frequently traveled. This path has many twists and turns ahead, and together we'll explore what this will mean for you. Reflect upon what you hope for your family now and in the future as you work together to create your family identity. You can do this together and separately as individuals. Once you've thought through these hopes, come back together to set goals that will help direct your energies. Expect differing emotions and experiences for each family member along the way. Regardless of your past, you're here now, creating a new family.

Define Your Family

Everyone faces adjustments as your family shifts. If you're the biological parent, you'll be balancing your new partner, your children, and any potential children you and your partner have. You'll also be responsible for setting the bar for your new family regarding expectations of respect, communication, and fun. Your expectations will affect not only your immediate family, but your extended family and your children's other biological parent as well. Though this will be a team effort by you and your partner, you'll see throughout this book that the biological parent is ultimately in the driver's seat. Your children will always look to you to lead. If both partners are bringing in children from previous relationships, then you will each be the head of your respective family unit.

Writing down your thoughts, questions, and imagined future will go a long way toward helping you develop a plan for your blended family. Grab some paper and a pen or pencil.

Biological parents, spend some time thinking and journaling about these questions:

- How do you want everyone to come together?

- What role will you take on in the next year?

- How do you imagine the dynamics of your blended family changing in the next five years?

- What role do you want your partner to take?

- What do you want to bring from your relationship with your children's other biological parent into your new relationship? What do you want to avoid?

As a stepparent, your job will be equally as tricky as your new partner's. You'll be learning how to live with not just one new person, but *several*. Your partner is a package deal—this is probably one of the reasons you fell in love with them. At the same time, there will be challenges. If you don't have children of your own, walking into a ready-made family can be exciting and intimidating. You'll be looking to your partner to help guide you in relating to your new stepkids, as you learn your role in their lives. Kids don't necessarily need more parents. They will, however, always need more stable, caring, considerate adults who value and respect them. If you have biological children of your own, you'll be trying to balance your time and attention so that all the kids in your home feel seen.

Stepparents, consider and write about these questions:

- How and where will you fit into the family structure?

- What guidance would you like from your partner?

- What are you worried about as you take on an instant family? What excites you?

- What do you hope for your relationship with your new stepkids?

- What support do you have outside the family to keep you afloat on difficult days?

Each of you can think about the following questions. Share your answers. Communication will be the glue that keeps your family boat together when the seas get rough. Even if the skies are clear now, even if you believe they will always stay clear, your survival depends on your boat.

Think of this adjustment period with three main support points:

1. Be honest and check in with yourself often to gauge how you're feeling.

2. Support one another as a couple and as a family. This means be fully open to hearing difficult feelings and celebrating accomplishments.

3. Focus on the children and what family situation will help them grow up happy.

Defining your new family requires support from all members, including your children. Discuss with your kids what their hopes and fears are surrounding moving in and blending together. How do they envision this situation? What would help them feel more comfortable? You can do this at a family meeting or by creating a "family vision board." Get a big poster board, markers, scissors, and glue. You can pull out old magazines to cut out words and images or print some pictures for each family member to contribute to the board. Working together, arrange images and words to depict your hopes for the family. You can get as creative as you'd like, but keep your focus on having fun and bonding as a family.

You can also talk individually with your biological or step-children, depending on the relationships and your comfort levels. You may find kids, especially older ones, struggle with participating in conversations like these. Taking a step back and asking them how they feel about the changes can be useful. Perhaps they aren't ready to talk about what the family will be like because they aren't ready to be a family yet. If this happens, do your best to create space to allow that experience for them. We'll talk more about working with emotions in this chapter (see pages 10–15).

Forcing everyone to feel like a family does not a family make. Family comes from laughter, positive experiences, effort, thoughtfulness, and time. Fights that clarify perspectives and help steer us in the right direction are also sometimes part of the family experience. One of the most essential pieces of bringing a family together is working to create a sense of belonging for everyone. What helps you feel like you've found your place in the world? How can you support this sense for your family?

For instance, my husband and stepdaughter, who was three at the time, told a story of a king who fell in love and brought a new queen into his castle to be a family with him and his little prin-cess. The age of your children will make a big difference in how you approach the topics throughout this book. The message, regardless of age, will remain the same: Focus on love, communi-cation, empathy, consistency, and respect. You can communicate your definition of the new family to others more effectively once you agree on what's important to you.

Set Goals

One way to get your partnership on the right path is to set family intentions. Using the questions from the previous section (see pages 3–4), engage with your partner about your priorities as you move forward together. As you read through this book, you might find your priorities shift or become clearer. Set tentative goals to start, and work toward being on the same page. Your goals or intentions could be in bullet format, a story of how things will look in the future, or a letter to your future selves. It is best to write your goals down and store them somewhere safe. You can revisit them whenever you need a reminder.

As you've learned from watching your children grow, you don't typically notice their changes from day to day. When you haven't seen a friend's baby in a few weeks, you're blown away by how much they've grown. When you experience your family day in and day out, you may not notice small but significant changes. This is why you want to write down your hopes and objectives for your family. Write about where you are now and what, for you, would be an indication of successful blending. You can make your goals measurable by creating a 1 to 10 scale for each objective.

After six months, check in by sitting down with your own goals, exploring progress with your partner, and getting curious about how your kids are feeling about the family coming together. Are you on the right track? If things haven't improved as you'd hoped, this will give you the opportunity to examine how you've gotten where you are before too much time has passed. Do more of what works, less of what doesn't. Since the period of time is only six months, make your goals or intentions reachable. Don't plan on having a fully blended, peaceful existence with everyone moving naturally around one another. Set your expectations for the long-term. According to Patricia Papernow, Ed.D., four to seven years is the amount of time to expect your blended family to function and feel like a family. If you strive to be perfect or push things along faster than the family members are ready to do so, you'll come up empty-handed. Instead, look for incremental change. However small, any forward movement is still success.

When you're looking to set goals for your family, remember that you cannot create something new while also holding on to everything you had before. Be sure to focus your goals on positive outcomes in *your* home, rather than a wish for something negative to go away. This includes being cognizant that everyone in your family is trying to be happy, and adjusting your goals to include each member. If you're struggling to come up with goals, look for something that would simply relieve some stress or pressure for you, and work from there.

Prioritize Your Children

If you are reading this book, your children have most likely been through some big adjustments, and now they're in for more. Keep their hearts in your mind as you move forward. As life-changing and wonderful as some of these events are, your kids probably had no say in any of them. They didn't get to choose when or under what circumstances their lives would change. Seeing this innocence will help you remain compassionate as you consider how to include the children in this transition.

During stressful times, remembering where children are coming from can be difficult. If they're struggling, their behavior or attitude can feel like obstinacy, rudeness, or a lack of caring.

You may also see regressive behavior or kids suddenly acting younger than their age. This could mean taking steps back in potty training, needing more glasses of water at bedtime, or asking you to do things for them that they previously were able to do on their own. You might also see more defiance, withdrawn behavior, or jealousy. Kids don't often know how to identify or express their emotions. Begin to think about what emotions could be underlying the behaviors you're seeing and feeling.

As an adult, you are responsible for supporting your children. Listening to them, considering their feelings in your decisions, and including them when appropriate is your job. You are tasked with not only trying to keep up with your own needs, but theirs as well. Children should never be responsible for their parents' needs. You can, of course, ask them for help with their younger siblings from time to time or with chores around the house, but keep in mind you'll need to listen to how they feel about helping and whether helping at this time is more than they can carry emotionally.

A common misstep parents make is to confuse their own role with their children or struggle with maintaining healthy boundaries. Parents may share too much or provide age-inappropriate information, include children in disagreements, attempt to communicate through their children to the other biological parent, or begin to think of their children as friends. Because of the power differential between parents and minor children, a healthy friendship and a healthy parent relationship cannot coexist. When a parent engages their children as friends, that parent loses sight of the role they play as a parent. Children have plenty of possibilities ahead of them for friendship. The same is not true regarding parents. For the benefit of your children, you're tasked with putting aside your feelings about your ex-spouse.

One of the easiest ways to prioritize your children is to recognize they are already going through a lot of change, so make any necessary adjustments gradually. Work to introduce them slowly to the blended family and anticipate they will need a little extra love, consideration, and support throughout this time. You'll be working to balance your children's needs for attention and connection with the excitement and effort you put toward your relationship.

EXAMPLES OF FAMILY SUCCESS

- Your stepchild decides to ride in the car with *you* when you and the biological parent drive separately.

- You find stepsiblings playing together peacefully and without prompting.

- You and your new partner work together to smooth over a difficult situation.

- Your stepchild asks you for help with homework or a problem with a friend.

- Your family gets to enjoy a full visit without any tantrums.

- Your shy biological children or stepchildren open up to you about their feelings.

Expect Emotions

Learning how to navigate your kids' big emotions is imperative. Expect that they will come to the table with their own experiences and feelings. You'll be able to anticipate some, others may take you by surprise. Here are a few scenarios of the kinds of experiences your kids may be having and what to do about them.

Your kids may still be mourning the loss of their biological parents being together. If you were never married or have been separated for years, you may be wondering why they're still dwelling on this. As common as divorce and blended families are, kids still feel the pressure and the wish for what could have been. They may still be holding on to hope that their parents will get back together. I remember my stepdaughter, all of five years old, once asked if her mom could live with us so she could have her whole family together. To her, that was a reasonable request. *Kids don't understand adult dynamics. Nor should they.* Our job is to listen to these statements with a full heart and to express empathy. What are our children really trying to tell us? What I heard from my stepdaughter was, "Hey guys? I'm sad and confused. I always miss who I'm not with, and I wish it could be easier." They're trying to tell us what they need, but kids speak a different language. Becoming fluent in child-speak is our job. Listen for the underlying message and respond to it. You can use reflections like, "You really wish your whole family could be under one roof, huh?" or open-ended questions like, "What's it like for you to have your mom and dad living in different homes?"

Your kids may be uncertain about how they're supposed to feel about their new family and the ways they'll fit in. They could be getting messages that tell them not to like their stepfamily.

This gets really confusing when they *do* actually like their step-family. Are they supposed to be in allegiance with one family over the other? Will they be betraying their other biological parent if they decide to feel happy in their new home? Imagine, then, if they don't like their new stepfamily. Maybe the new parent has a different parenting style, stepsiblings have new personalities that change the atmosphere, or they're struggling to share their time and attention with this new family. They could have fear rumbling in their tummies—*Is there enough love to go around?* These existential feelings are too big for kids to process on their own. Try your best to help relieve what pressure you can for them. You'll hear this over and over: Communication is key. Check in with your kids daily. What was their favorite part of the day? What feelings are they struggling with? Find fun ways to help them release negative energy. Have 30-second dance parties where you shake the energy away. Blow bubbles and imagine placing any problems into the bubbles so you can watch them float away and disappear.

Whatever feelings your children are bringing to you, meet them with empathy, communication, and connection. Like you, your children may feel any number of emotions: anxiety, anger, confusion, fear of abandonment. When these feelings come up, listen to understand, not to correct or fix an immediate issue. Reflect what you hear to make sure you got the right message. Express that you can understand why they might feel that way, and comfort them by telling them how significant they are to you and how much their parents love them. With older kids, ask them what might help. Kids do best when they feel seen, valued, and considered. They need consistency and reliability, so let's give them consistent messages, reliably showing up and creating space for their feelings and needs.

Your children look to the adults in the family—you, your partner, their other biological parent, and any other adults in their lives—for how to manage and express emotions. You may not have control over how emotions are dealt with at their other home, but you do in yours. If you get frustrated and yell, slam objects down, or check out emotionally, then don't be surprised when they do the same thing. If you never show or share your feelings, how will they know the best ways to manage their own?

One of the greatest gifts you'll receive and burdens you'll face as a parent is the need to be at your best with constant effort toward growing and improving. If you're not currently equipped with a wide range of emotional understanding, including ways of feeling emotions and expressing them appropriately, then working with your children's emotions will begin with work on your own. It helps if your children see that you also have happiness, sadness, frustration, and fear. Don't share with them like they're your best friends, but you can give them glimpses into your world to help normalize theirs. "Mom is feeling pretty sad today. That's okay, we all feel sad at times. When I feel sad, my chest feels heavy, I get a lump in my throat, and my eyes tear up. I thought I might go for a walk later since that usually helps. What helps when you're feeling sad?"

You might notice as you work to help your children navigate their emotions that you feel the reemergence of some of your own emotional wounds. Perhaps you struggled with not ever feeling like you lived up to your dad's expectations, your mother was emotionally absent, or you went through your own difficult times during your parents' divorce. You might feel old anxieties creep up as you build a new relationship after an old relationship ended. You are allowed to have feelings and to struggle. Processing your own emotional experience is as important as the

"Communication will be the glue that keeps your family boat together when the seas get rough."

rest of the family processing theirs. Acknowledging the issues you faced is also your responsibility so your children don't carry the same wounds as they grow. If your children see you experience a full spectrum of emotions, this can help them normalize highly emotional situations and learn how to cope. They should never be saddled, though, with the burden of caring for you. Your job is to manage your own trauma so that your children are not impacted. If you find yourself stuck in inconsolable crying episodes, paralyzed by anxiety, or exhibiting long-lasting anger outbursts, seeking out more support may be a good idea.

Sometimes kids need a safe space that's just for them. A place where they're not trying to live up to real or imagined expectations of one or both of their parents. Individual therapy can do wonders for children and teens. For children 12 years old and younger, look for a registered play therapist. You can find therapists through the Association for Play Therapy. These counselors are trained to work within the children's natural language: play. As kids get older, they often engage partly in play and partly in processing verbally. Even with teens, these therapists often use games and art to help them feel more comfortable in the room so they can talk through their feelings. Another great resource for kids is a support group where they can see they are not the only ones whose biological parents aren't together. You may be able to find a support group through your school counselor, local community mental health center, or a private practitioner.

THE *DOS* AND *DON'TS* OF REACTING TO KIDS' STRONG FEELINGS

DO: Reflect empathy. To express empathy, you must first feel your way into it. Imagine a time when you felt similarly: left out, confused, overwhelmed, or scared. Then communicate that you care, are listening, and see them.

DON'T: Ignore children reaching out. Children seek attention for a reason. Think of this behavior as children reaching out for connection. Everyone needs connection to thrive.

DO: Stay present and lean in during tough times. Time-outs are for adults to take when adults need to relax and breathe. Time-ins are for stepping into children's emotions with them, to teach regulation skills. You want them to see that you love them no matter what they feel.

DON'T: Expect kids to stay the same. Everyone and everything else is changing. Kids may regress, or become shy and quiet, or outgoing and boisterous. Greet them as they are.

Settling into Your New Home

One last aspect as we get started is to think about how you plan to settle into your new home. Are you moving into one partner's already established home or creating a new one together? How might your children feel if someone new comes into their space or if they go into someone else's space? You'll want to consider what their room is going to look like, how their space might change, and what their comfort level is. Take special care with children who tend to find comfort and safety at home. Will they need to share their room with a stepsibling? Will they need to move over a little to allow more space for the incoming family members? Will you create a special space just for the kids?

As we've been discussing, incremental changes will be your friend. If you move all their stuff over in one swift movement, the shock may be too big. At the same time, if you move one part of their life week after week, they may begin to feel like the flux will continue indefinitely until there is no longer room for them. Kids are particularly sensitive to their space and belongings. It doesn't take much for them to feel threatened, invisible, or treated unfairly. They thrive when they feel you care about their place in the home and make efforts to show it. Talk with your kids in advance about what will need to change and how you plan to make those changes, so they have time to adjust. Involve them in the process if they're open to doing so, and have them come up with creative ideas to incorporate everyone.

If you have never lived with small children, you may be used to having certain decor around the home, including furnishings, art, and knickknacks wherever you wish. Do yourself a favor and decorate your new home together with the children in mind. With small children, you may want to put away any particularly nostalgic items. If you've always had a pristine white couch, you may want to look at other options or prepare yourself emotionally for the couch to lose its color or shape. If your partner is new to children, they may need a kid-free portion of the house. If you can have a dedicated toy room or bins to help make cleanup a breeze, do so. Making a plan in advance will help everyone feel more at home in the family's shared space.

You may also be facing some wars about that ugly old furniture you've held dear all these years. Keep in the forefront of your mind that you are working to build something together. This means a willingness to make space for one another. You are teammates, not competitors, when it comes to your relationship, including rearranging and decorating your home so everyone feels comfortable. The adjustment to living together can be long, and some families find after years they still haven't figured it out. Don't fret—now is a good time to revisit any issues about living together that need to be addressed. Keep the conversation going. What works in the home now might not work in five years.

Also consider what your setup will be for your partnership. How will you find time and space for the two of you as you settle in together? Perhaps you can create a cozy corner for the kids and have a nice couple of chairs on your patio to drink tea at night and check in with one another as a couple. Just as you are mindful to set up a comfortable environment for your children, so you should consciously create a couple's space. Most importantly, have fun when dreaming and setting up your home. Make a place you want to live, that reflects the both of you, and something to help you feel excited to build your family.

CHAPTER TWO

A New Partnership

Blended families start one way: Two people—one or both with at least one child already—decide to bring their lives together. Though we've discussed how the biological parent will be the one who leads their children through this journey, the couple sets the tone for the family. Without the couple, there is no blended family. With all the love, care, and work you have already put in and that is still ahead of you, this point must be clear: Your relationship as a couple is paramount to the health and happiness of the family. It will need to be cared for and prioritized to remain strong. Let's talk about how to make that happen.

Define Your Relationship

Understanding how you and your partner feel about the relationship and what each person expects from it is vital to the health of any partnership. The purpose of relationships has evolved over time. What was once a partnership of convenience, wealth, and shared work has become a partnership for emotional support, spiritual growth, and a deep abiding connection. Be authentic with one another about what you hope to gain from the relationship.

Every couple must find their own groove. For some couples, this means that one person stays home to care for the children and the house while the other makes most or all of the money. If this is your intention, you'll have to look at how this will impact your couple relationship as well as your relationship with your children. Will the kids be staying home with their biological parent or stepparent? How will you engage as a team and avoid feeling like one person carries the weight of the family?

In other couples, both parents work. Sometimes that means paying for babysitters or daycare; other times, maintaining opposite schedules to keep childcare costs down. If you're both working and both responsible for the home and children, how will you divide your time, efforts, and tasks? How will you carve out time together if you're faced with opposite schedules? Look for compromises that help both people feel their needs are met. If you're a morning person and your partner is a night owl, perhaps you wake up with the kids and your partner can put them to bed.

The invisible burden of motherhood is a real phenomenon in our culture. In many homes, both parents want or need to work. Yet, expectations of generations past haven't fully worn off, and there is often still the expectation that women carry the primary load of caring for the children and the home. Sometimes this looks like the mother taking on the management of the family: making doctor's appointments, chaperoning school events, delegating chores, purchasing household items, and managing the family calendar. If only one person takes on all these tasks when both partners work, disaster is around the corner. The best partners in dual working homes (if not most homes) are the ones who take an active role in their children's lives. They engage with them, carry half the management load, and don't approach their role as "helping their partners," or, "watching the children." This is infinitely more applicable when they are the one who brings children from previous relationships.

Chores, money, and parenting are some of the most frequent and pervasive topics of argument for couples. As you're working together to define your partnership and family, keep in mind that you may not be able to solve all these issues. The goal, then, is to get skilled at talking about them. Even if a compromise comes easily, your life will continue to evolve, and you must adapt as time goes on. What works now may not work when you have another child, live in another home, or get another job. Satisfaction in relationships happens when both people are on the same page.

One last part of defining your relationship is looking at what you believe to be the point of your relationship. To accomplish this, you'll each need to spend some time alone exploring your own thoughts, feelings, and expectations. Think about past relationships and what worked and didn't work for you. Consider your future and how you hope the relationship will evolve over time. Then focus on the present: what you love about your partner, what brings you closer to them, and how you feel when you're together. Sitting down in a quiet, comfortable place may help get genuine answers from your wisest self. Maybe that's in your living room, in nature, or at a coffee shop. Writing those answers down may help, or if you're feeling creative, draw a picture instead. Once you have each spent some time thinking through your expectations of the relationship, sit down to share them. We'll go into greater depth in the next section (see pages 24–26) about how to make the most of these conversations. Start by recounting the story of how you fell in love.

When your partner shares their hopes with you, keep your focus on building your future together. You're not looking for where their hopes or expectations differ from or conflict with yours. Instead, look for what they need and consider which aspects will be easy for you to meet and which will be a challenge. Relationships are difficult in themselves, and adding a blended family to the equation makes them more so. Anything you can do to keep your mind focused on the positive aspects of the relationship sets you up for success long-term.

KEY POINTS TO CONSIDER AND DISCUSS

- **Money:** Who will pay for what in the relationship? Will you combine your finances, keep them completely separate, or blend the two? Will the finances for the children be split evenly, regardless of biological relation, or divided? How do you know what's fair?

- **Household:** How will you find the balance for housework and parenting? Will one person take on the bulk of the load? Are there chores you like doing? Who has the higher standard for cleanliness? Will you expect the kids to help?

- **Relationship:** What does being in a romantic relationship mean? What is most important to you—a best friend, someone who challenges you, or someone who backs you up? Do you plan to be monogamous? What helps you feel connected to your partner?

- **Marriage, Babies, and More:** Are you married or do you want to be? Do you want more children together? How can you balance individual needs versus the needs of the family? What would be a sign that your relationship is doing well—or struggling?

Communicate Clearly and Completely

Communicate, communicate, communicate. That's one of the first pieces of advice people offer at a wedding. But what exactly does communicating mean? There are three key components to communication for your blending family and relationship. You can think of them as the heart, the head, and the hand.

The first is to listen to each other. A little obvious, I know, but not as simple as it may sound. More than just lending an ear, listening requires your full, undivided attention to pay attention to more than words. When you're trying to listen to your partner, as much as you might genuinely wish to hear them out, you might also find your mind wandering. You might start to plan your response while they're still talking, get distracted by a rotating mental to-do list, or get caught up in assuming what they're going to say next. If you're doing these things, you're not really listening. You know when you've been listened to because you feel a deeper connection. You're met with empathy, or the willingness for someone to tap into their own experience to better understand yours. You feel seen and accepted as you are, whether or not the other person agrees with your position. The same goes for your partner. Once they feel listened to, they're more likely to fully listen in return. Listening in this way is the *heart* of communication.

Once you understand where someone is coming from, you have an opportunity. You can genuinely consider their position or simply argue your own. Considering others is a vulnerable choice, requiring your willingness to be wrong and resist the urge to dig your heels into your perspective. People have the tendency to get so focused on winning fights, they lose sight of their point: the happiness and health of the relationship. *You can*

always be accountable in your interactions and relationships.
Even if only two percent of the issue is your fault, you still must
own that. Seeing when you've hurt someone you love can be
painful, which makes acknowledging your part all the more difficult. There is no shame in recognizing the hurt. Guilt helps you
learn and improve. It helps your partner and relationship heal.
You are not responsible for how other people react to situations,
but you are responsible for communicating in a respectful way,
including being honest, kind, and purposeful with your speech.
You are responsible for responding with awareness and intention to your partner's reactions and looking for any sign that
your intended message may have been lost. If you might have
sent the wrong message, hurt them, or were unfair, take accountability. When others take accountability, you are more likely to
meet them with the same. When you recognize your options,
acknowledge your impact on others, and look at the situation
with a balanced mind, you are using the *head* of communication.

Now let's put your newfound knowledge into action—the
hand of communication. Allowing your love for your partner
to impact your decisions and behaviors is a sign of a secure,
trusting relationship. Integrating each other's perspectives helps
you grow stronger individually and as a unit. If your partner is
a homebody and you thrive on social interactions, you'll have to
find a middle ground that meets both people's comfort levels. If
you're busy with family and friends for several days, know that
you'll need to carve out some alone time to keep your partner
sane. Like everything in relationships, a little give-and-take goes
a long way. The healthiest relationships come from both people
feeling seen, respected, and accepted for who they are.

As a blended family, your ability as partners to listen to,
consider, and integrate each other's perspectives is even more

important than for couples who don't already have children. Having defined your relationship at this point is helpful, as different setups can bring different communication strategies. For example, couples who are simply dating tend to fight as part of figuring out whether their relationship can last for the long haul. Once you've already decided your relationship will last, the fighting shifts. You start to fight *for* the improvement of the relationship, knowing that you'll be waking up next to your partner every morning from here on out.

Create a Co-Parenting Unit

There are suddenly a lot of adults in your family, and getting everyone working together can be a process. As a blended couple, forces outside your home will impact your relationship more so than in a first-time family or a couple without children. You'll be navigating the tricky waters in your own home while blending your family. Simultaneously, everyone in your home will be impacted in both positive and challenging ways by your ex-spouses. How you balance working together as a couple and as a parenting unit will shape how your relationship fares over time.

As mentioned before, differences in parenting styles are some of the top reasons couples fight. Our family culture pumps through our veins, coloring our view of the world. The way your parents raised you—including strategies, expectations, and traditions—shaped who you are today. Disagreements that crop up are often because each person feels like their parents did it the right way, even when they didn't particularly like the way they were raised. Still, your brain and heart will assume your experience is what is normal. This is how intergenerational patterns persist: You are doing the best you can with what you have. Your job is to keep learning and gaining the tools needed for success. Anything outside of what you're accustomed to will feel uncomfortable. Here's the great part: If you are uncomfortable, you are probably changing, being challenged, stretching, or growing. Did you ever have your legs hurt as a kid, only to shoot up an inch seemingly overnight? Growing pains. Your heart and mind experience them, too.

THE *DOS* AND *DON'TS* OF CO-PARENTING

DO: Use phrases like these when answering questions the kids ask: "Have you already asked (other parent)?" or "Let me check in with (other parent) and get back to you."

DON'T: Override the other parent's boundaries or requests. If you do so accidentally, acknowledge the mistake to the kids and follow through with the original request.

DO: Talk each evening about how the day went, including where you got stuck, what successes you had, and how you felt about your teamwork.

DON'T: Correct the other person's parenting in front of the children. If your partner seems to be getting overwhelmed, you can ask them to take a break or set up a tag-teaming plan ahead of time.

And you will face growing pains as you bring two families together. If you're both bringing kids into the situation, you've probably each grown accustomed to how the other does things. Not only will you have to adjust to your partner's ways, but they'll have to adjust to yours. Look at your differences. Acknowledge and respect them, and then look for what benefits your partner brings. If you're great with boundaries and your partner is loads of fun, then you each have something to learn. Whereas your partner could learn to set more consistent limits and routines, you could relax and enjoy your kids more. There's always room for improvement.

If only one of you is bringing a child or children into the family, you have a different set of circumstances to navigate. The parent will be used to living their lives in their own groove with their children, and the new stepparent won't yet have a fully developed parenting identity. The stepparent will go from a life without the responsibility of children to an instant family. That loss of freedom can be a difficult adjustment for the stepparent, and it may take time to fully realize what this means. As the biological parent, you must continue to assume 100% of the responsibility for parenting. Your new partner is there to help support you, but not to assume your responsibilities. Stepparents will need to ease into their role in the family for the benefit of the children, the relationship, and each individual parent. Of course, as their relationship with the children improves, any support they can offer the biological parent, including some self-care time, will be invaluable.

If you're a new stepparent, you may still be exploring how you want to be as a parent, but that doesn't mean you don't have valuable skills and insights to bring. Over time, the goal is the same as if you both have children: to learn from one another. The biological parent can always learn from new, fresh perspectives. The stepparent will also learn as they integrate feedback for what does and doesn't work with the kids.

Making sure you understand each other's expectations of co-parenting will be crucial. In chapter 3, we'll go in more depth about how to set up rules, discipline, and decisions, but in terms of the health of your relationship, your expectations for each other can lift you up or weigh you down. A couple who agrees about their expectations and can talk them through, making adjustments when they get too high or low, is set up for success. This couple will meet one another with curiosity and kindness. They'll be thoughtful of one another, concerned about their partner's well-being, and focused on building healthy relationships among all family members so each person can thrive.

Regardless of the situation, your ultimate goal in co-parenting is to be a united force, a solid unit who approaches the children as a team, not two people who can be played against each other. This will require trust and commitment to working together through the challenges you face. View any disagreements or stuck feelings as opportunities to create a deeper connection. Take a step toward the other person. You are both trying to make the situation as positive and loving as possible—you may just be trying to take different paths to get there.

Understanding Boundaries

Navigating boundaries in a blended family takes some getting used to. As a couple, you'll be relying on each other to help find the way through learning each family member's boundaries, as well as creating the expectations for the family in general. Boundaries play an integral role in setting up healthy relationships—as a couple and as a parenting unit. First, let's understand the role of boundaries.

Boundaries help us define how we want to shape our space, how we speak and act toward others, and how we allow others' words and actions to affect us. There are two types of boundaries: internal and external. Internal boundaries stipulate how we allow others to affect us emotionally. If someone says something mean, do you take it to heart? Or does nothing penetrate? External boundaries are how we navigate the space between people. Some people hug nearly everyone they meet, whereas others walk around with a larger personal bubble. We tend to recognize external boundaries more easily than the more subtle internal ones.

External boundaries are often more straightforward. We typically know when someone is too close to our body. One activity to try with the family is to have each person, one at a time, walk slowly toward another family member. When the standing person feels the walking one is close enough, they say stop. The other person stops walking. Then you can talk about how each feels when the other takes one step closer or farther away. Take turns so each family member has the opportunity to set and feel boundaries from all other members. Watching how this changes over time as relationships grow closer is interesting.

Internal boundaries are often learned by bumping into them. Have you ever had someone say something in passing that you end up carrying around for years? That is a loose internal boundary: You took what they said to heart, perhaps without realizing it. Relying on open and honest communication about boundaries, and being willing to hear when you've inadvertently crossed one, helps you work through these issues as your family gets accustomed to living with one another.

"Satisfaction in relationships happens when both people are on the same page."

Boundaries can be too tight as well as too loose. The too-tight boundaries tend to come across as strict, inflexible, or aloof. Those that are too loose, then, reflect just the opposite. They're free-flowing, overly flexible, or uncertain, and can lead to sharing too much too soon. Healthy boundaries live in the gray area between these two extremes: There is structure, but also some flexibility when appropriate. They represent a balance between understanding each person's comfort levels and making adjustments and accommodations when needed.

To communicate your boundaries to others—whether those boundaries relate to emotions, material goods, or personal space—you must first know your own boundaries. Spend some time thinking about whether you're comfortable setting boundaries or if you allow people to cross your comfort levels more than you'd like. Where can you improve? Knowing this helps you engage more honestly and prevents arguments down the road.

A key tip: *If you're angry, frustrated, overwhelmed, or otherwise upset within a relationship, you probably need to set a boundary with yourself or someone else.* Use your feelings as reminders to guide you in learning your own boundaries.

As a stepparent, you may need to learn to knock on your teenager's door before entering, to allow your two-year-old to choose their own spoon, and to take a backseat when your partner needs to set a limit. You haven't been with the children since birth, so you won't instinctively know these boundaries yet. If you hear the words, "you're not my mother/father," or trigger a smaller child's meltdown, take some deep breaths and remain calm. If you're the stepparent, they are right—you are not their mother or father. Listen to what they are saying. You might initially hear them acting out with defiance, but perhaps underneath, they're trying to tell you that you stepped on a boundary. Back up, see if you can calmly figure out what the boundary was, take accountability, and apologize. Then explain your experience of the situation.

This is where you'll need to rely on your partner and your relationship. If you as the biological parent see your partner has inadvertently stepped on a boundary of your child's or the family's, your job is to kindly and gently help your partner recognize what they've done and to learn from the experience. If you notice that something feels strange between you, speak up. Keep your eye on exploring each other's comfort levels and get good at talking through the awkward moments.

Body safety is another kind of boundary that's essential to discuss as a couple. Who is allowed to help younger kids with diapers, dressing, and bathing? Do you have an open-door policy when kids are playing in bedrooms? Do you practice body-safe practices like not forcing physical affection and not keeping secrets? There are great resources from organizations like Parenting Safe Children that can help guide these conversations (see the Resources section on page 125). Make sure the kids know they are each responsible for their own bodies and to respect not only themselves, but one another.

Learning your own needs, understanding what others need, engaging in discussions around these needs, and working together to help everyone feel comfortable takes time. This is a work in progress. All of this won't be perfect, but it doesn't have to be. You'll learn from one another and increase your connection through your day-to-day interactions.

Managing Money

No matter who they are or what their background is, most people never quite feel like they have enough money. An endless reach for more income tends to be met with bigger bills and responsibilities. Figuring out how to divide the money in a blended home can help partners feel equal in their shared responsibilities and keep resentments from building. In your family, this might mean that one person makes most, if not all, of the money whereas the other contributes in other ways. In other homes, both partners work outside the home and contribute to finances. Regardless of your setup, everyone needs to feel respected for the ways they contribute and comfortable knowing the necessities are met.

AS A COUPLE

Being a couple starts with communication. Having the ability to communicate about finances without getting into heated arguments is necessary for long-term stability. As you figure out finances, remember that you're a team. Start with a discussion to better understand each other's spending, saving, and credit use habits. If one person tends to spend a little more frivolously while the other squirrels away their pennies, you'll need to set up a different situation than if each of you is careful with your money. When you get married, all your partner's debt becomes your debt, too. Knowing about the situation ahead of time is best, but learning about the debt later is better than not knowing about it at all. Be transparent with each other. You'll need to discuss finances for the rest of your lives together, so there's no time like the present to start.

How you divide your income and pay your bills will be up to you. Some couples pool all their money together into one bank account and pay for everything from that account. Others share the financial burden of paying bills, and still others have one person primarily responsible for the coming and going of money. Regardless of the setup you choose, I highly recommend monthly sit-downs to review the numbers and know where you stand. I've seen some couples in blended families feel the need to keep their finances private from each other. If you're married, working through that urge to be private and instead working toward transparency is worth the effort. If finances are not your strong suit, you can use online templates, and if you have the means to hire professional financial planners to help with retirement or taxes, do so. You'll have to ask yourself and your partner questions like:

- Who saves for retirement?

- Will you work together to get out of debt?

- Is each person's debt their own responsibility?

- Will you file taxes together? Separately?

- Who saves up and pays for family travel? How?

- Who pays for dinners out versus groceries, and how do you keep track?

- How much do you each contribute to a rainy day fund?

- Are you living in the house of one partner? Who pays for decorations? What about repairs?

I've seen a few options for splitting finances equally, and they each have their selling points. One is to gather the household bills and divide them by two, regardless of how much each person makes. Then, any personal bills are paid with what's left. What you put in savings depends on what remains after all bills and entertainment. This can work fairly easily when each member of the couple has similar income and debts. Less math, fewer headaches. In a slight variation of this system, the couple pools their money and pays all their household and personal bills together, then equally splits whatever is left of the combined funds. The other option is for couples whose income is more uneven, or when one or both partners are bogged down by debt. In this scenario, the couple takes their combined total income and finds what percentage each person makes. That percentage is how much of the household bills they pay. You can include personal debt if you wish. Some couples do and some don't. At the end of the day, both people should have similar amounts of money left over.

AS PARENTS

Once you figure out who owes what, makes what, and pays what, you can look at how you pay for your children. If you split custody fifty-fifty, you most likely are not receiving any money from your ex-spouse. If you have a different arrangement and are receiving support, that money should be used to pay for the needs of your children. In the event child support payments do not cover half of the cost of raising your children, you, as a couple, will need to sit down and have a heart-to-heart about how you want to cover child expenses. For instance, financial planners typically don't automatically include stepchildren in calculations for life insurance. Ask yourself and your partner these kinds of questions:

- Do you wish to pay for your own children?

- Do you feel the cost should be shared?

- With life insurance, who carries what and who are the beneficiaries?

- Do you leave money behind for your stepchildren?

- Do your assets all go to your partner or to your biological children?

I ultimately recommend that families keep finances for the children as the responsibility of the biological parent, who should be splitting the child expenses with the other biological parent. In theory, the biological parent and children could support themselves before the stepparent entered the picture. Of course, there are cases when this isn't possible, including when the other biological parent is absent or has passed away. If the stepparent chooses to help when they're able, that can make the couple feel stronger together. The biological parent, however, should not rely on that income to sustain the children's expenses. If the stepparent is not helping voluntarily, resentment can build quickly. Of course, expenses for any children you have together should be split equally according to how you figured out the rest of your finances.

Ultimately, the way you combine finances should be something with which you are both comfortable. Setting up a financial situation that works for you will require vulnerable talks about your past with money, the spending habits that get you stuck, and your hopes for your financial future. It also means talking about what would happen if you split up or when you die. These topics aren't typically a favorite to discuss, but they are all the more important in blended families. Separation can be more complex when there are stepchildren, shared children, and previous divorce rulings to consider. Throughout these conversations, focus on teamwork, managing the comfort levels of both partners, and ways to keep your family happy and healthy in the long run.

THE *DOS* AND *DON'TS* OF NAVIGATING BOUNDARIES

DO: Advocate for your needs. Assertive boundaries are easier to respect.

DON'T: Guilt children into wanting to engage in a relationship with you, including with physical affection. You'll gain their respect by respecting them.

DO: Work on your emotion regulation skills. You're more effective when you're able to notice when something bothers you. Relax a little and then set a boundary.

DON'T: Set a boundary in anger. If you're at your tipping point, walk away and take some space. You can later reapproach the topic and explain your experience.

DO: Keep in mind that internal boundaries are as important as external boundaries. You're in control of who and what penetrates your heart.

Keep Your Relationship Healthy

If you're feeling overwhelmed, know that you're not alone. There are millions of other couples working hard at this right alongside you. Your relationship as a couple, the two people bringing this family together, must be one of your highest priorities. Your blended family will not thrive if your relationship is not strong.

You may have heard the odds of successful marriages with children from previous relationships are relatively low, with divorce rates between 60% and 70%. Let this motivate you, not deter you. Let's look at some practices that help.

Close your eyes for a moment and bring to mind one of the first experiences of falling in love with your partner. Breathe into the feeling until it fills your chest with the warmth. Do this any time you find yourself frustrated, stuck, or unsure. That love is the purpose behind all this work. You're in this boat for a reason. Returning to this love over and over and nourishing it will help keep your relationship grounded. If you start to get lost in this practice, consider what love means for you. One definition I've appreciated over the years is that insecure love says, "I need you to make me happy." Secure love says, "I want you to be happy."

KEEP TALKING

Keep your communication open and ongoing. Talk things all the way through but take breaks when you need them. If you get overwhelmed in a conversation, try taking a break from the discussion—but not necessarily from the relationship—for an hour or two at minimum. After the break, instead of hoping the issue goes away on its own, you'll need to come back and finish the conversation. If you struggle to communicate face-to-face, try journaling to one another and exchanging notebooks. You can also try taking turns sharing, with five minutes of listening followed by two minutes of reflecting with no interruptions. Try not to text about delicate or heated topics. Texting becomes problematic for two reasons. First, we read text messages in our mind, in our voice, with the tone we assume our partner is taking. Our assumptions are not always correct. Second, when we text, not only do we assume we'll receive an immediate response (and can get testy when we don't), but we also quickly shoot off messages without putting our full intention into them.

When you have difficult discussions, seek to understand instead of desperately trying to be understood. If you recall from our discussion about healthy communication, really paying attention can be difficult. Listening to understand does more for the relationship than just helping you respond. It deepens your connection, breaks down barriers, and keeps you in a patient, open state.

YOU'RE IN THIS TOGETHER

When you're struggling to communicate, look at your partner with fresh eyes and keep things in perspective. What's the point of an argument? Are you trying to win? Are you hoping to be understood? Are you afraid you'll lose them? Be honest with your partner about how you're feeling. Brutal honesty is not so much the point, but rather a willingness to acknowledge your feelings and communicate with them, even when doing so makes you feel vulnerable. Too often partners skirt around an issue, make little jabs, use sarcasm, or just stew in their feelings. Though obvious, simply talking to your partner about something that's bothering you is something couples often forget or are afraid to do. Being honest doesn't mean you say what anger wants you to say. Being honest means saying what's underneath the anger.

Instead of, "Why do you have to be so stubborn?" try, "I'm scared we won't be able to solve this." Looking at your partner anew means letting go of the past and the assumptions between you so that you can really see them as they are, right now. Keep perspective by remembering your end goal: a happier, healthier relationship and family.

Find ways to connect as a couple each day, week, month, and year. Daily connections can be simple, like checking in with each other every night before you go to sleep. The Gottman Institute, which provides training and workshops to clinicians and couples and has been studying marriage for nearly four decades, suggests that a kiss that lasts at least six seconds increases connection. Try increasing the length of your hello and goodbye kisses and hugs to increase the release of connecting chemicals and hormones that reduce your stress. You can also use *The 5 Love Languages* by Gary Chapman to look for ways to show love to your partner in a "language" they can understand. The goal is to fill up each other's "love tanks," as he calls them. The Gottman Institute calls this the emotional bank account. But whether a bucket, tank, or bank account, the goal is the same: For each person to feel as though they and the relationship are in good order, they need something from which to draw. Our responsibility is both to fill our own reserves and contribute to our partner's. What separates successful and unsuccessful relationships is the care put into the regular day-to-day encounters and keeping the relationship a priority.

Weekly connections can range from date nights, to each person having a night to get some individual self-care time. Maybe you grab coffee together Saturday mornings or have Sunday dinners as a family. The weekly goal is to carve out quality time that helps build each person up and maintains the connection you share. Get interested in each other. Reminisce, dream about the future, or express gratitude for your life now.

Monthly connections are for refreshing any stale parts of a relationship. Kid-free dates are a must to keep your love alive and thriving. Find a great babysitter, a family member, or another couple in town (and you can do the same for them) to take care of the children a few times each month. To add variety to your dates, have each partner write down activities they would enjoy doing together. Research ideas online or ask your friends. Then, once a month (or more!) pull a date idea from the jar and start planning. Take turns initiating so both partners feel taken care of. During your monthly dates, see about incorporating deeper conversations and check-ins to keep your finger on the pulse of the relationship. Is it weak or strong? Does it skip a beat or is it rhythmic and smooth? Engaging in these conversations helps you stay authentic, vulnerable, and passionate with one another.

Yearly connections can be special evenings away where you splurge on something you love—these can happen more than once a year as well. Take long vacations to beaches or weekend staycations at home. Find ways to celebrate each other and the journey you're on together. These are particularly helpful if you've been letting your relationship stagnate on the back burner. However, these planned connections aren't enough to keep a relationship happy for life. You must continue to nurture the relationship as the days and weeks pass.

One of the most contentious topics for couples is the level of satisfaction or dissatisfaction with their sex life. As with all other issues we've discussed, communication is how you move through issues in the bedroom. Physical intimacy is more than just sexual intercourse. Physical intimacy includes holding hands, hugs, snuggles on the couch, and a pat on the bottom as you walk past your partner in the kitchen. Foreplay happens all throughout the day as you consider, notice, and appreciate each other. Issues around sex typically stem from struggles with vulnerability and with wanting to feel loved. Couples often struggle with feeling that one partner holds the power for the sex in their marriage. Since most couples have different appetites, whoever has the lower libido tends to hold the power. Be conscious of this power and make efforts to dispel the difference. Conversations from the get-go about each partner's hopes and fears about frequency, desire, fidelity, and appetite will help in the present and in the future as you encounter some dry spells over the years.

Sexual deserts happen in most relationship journeys. What one couple considers a desert might be another couple's rainforest. One major barrier to intimacy in couples of blended families is stress. With children and stepchildren in the home, the ongoing effort and energy you put forth to make all the relationships work can wear on you over time. The uncertainty in rough times and the sense of not being on the same parenting page can pull you away from the intimacy your relationship needs to thrive. Use your communication skills to keep your connection. In these uncertain periods, seek to understand. Keep your closeness and intimacy at the forefront of your interactions. Perhaps most importantly, this part of your relationship is supposed to be fun! Laughter is a great way to bring couples closer in the bedroom.

DON'T BE AFRAID TO ASK FOR HELP

If you're struggling, there's no shame in seeking out a marriage counselor. I hear frequently from couples that they're worried that going to a counselor means the end of their marriage. The stigma behind this isn't without cause. Many couples who go to relationship counseling do not stay together. Pause that thought, though, because this is a situation of correlation, not causation. Many couples who come in wait until they're already at the point of divorce before they reach out for help. They often want a quick fix to decades of hurt and aren't always willing to face what's required to revive the marriage. The best option? Go to counseling at the first sign of trouble.

How do you know when to seek professional help? If you notice arguments that feel intense though the topic seems silly, are at a stalemate for two or more weeks, or start to feel like you're losing the closeness in the relationship, you might consider looking into counseling. Even when things are going well, engage in couples counseling, if only for a few sessions here and there, to check up on the relationship. This helps identify any potential issues and can give you skills to avoid future pitfalls. Keep going, at least periodically, throughout your relationship. Don't wait for years of resentment, disconnection, and pain to accumulate. If you're concerned, seek out a marriage-friendly therapist and keep the focus of your counseling on problem solving and reconnecting instead of blaming and trying to be the right one.

If you're both fully committed to being honest, respectful, loving, and vulnerable, there's always hope you can repair and revive your partnership. This process will take effort. You'll have to be honest about and face your inner demons, allow them to come into the open air, and trust that your partner will greet them gently. Choose to step out of your "me" space and meet each other in the "we" space. Lean in toward each other. Relationships are like their own person in the home. They need to be listened to, cared for, and considered. With effort, time, and care, your relationship can flourish. You can look at your partner most days and feel your love for them warm your body. You can be in love and raise a blended family at the same time.

CHAPTER THREE
A New Way to Parent

You and your partner will need to join forces to create a solid parenting unit. Both partners will be bringing their experiences and beliefs about parenting, and these beliefs may or may not align. The situation is a balancing act—recognizing your own responsibilities and parenting approach while incorporating new ideas from a partner who comes from a different upbringing. When you throw in ex-spouses, including uncooperative ones, you'll need to adjust your previous parenting styles. You'll find a new way to parent, together.

Acknowledge Your Feelings, Concerns, and Fears

To figure out where to go, you must first discover where you are. Acceptance is key to this process and is simply an acknowledgment of what is. Once you can accept who you are as parents, how you were raised, and your strengths and weaknesses, you're better able to find your next steps. Keeping the intention for acceptance in mind as you parse your feelings and learn those of your partner is essential.

Acceptance is particularly important for blending families. Even though modern families may not fit a set mold, in America you're often raised with a standard image of family: 2.5 children, white picket fence, golden retriever, biological parents happily married. Grieving differences in the ways you had envisioned your life, family, and home is normal, but accepting the way your life is will keep you from holding yourself accountable to expectations that don't apply to your family. You must create your own standards and expectations that apply to your unique situation, and you're most skilled in doing so when you acknowledge, or accept what is, and move forward with how your life is today. Keep your focus on what is within your control.

What is within your control? The answer is simple: *You* are. You have the power to learn, grow, and change as parents and people. To do that, you need to take a close look at how you're feeling and be honest with yourself and your partner about your experience. There are three things to consider within yourself before delving further into parenting discussions.

MANAGING STRESS

The first is to factor in how you handle stress. Managing stress is about recognizing what happens when you get overwhelmed. Knowing your automatic response to stress helps you anticipate potential snags and plan your coping skills in advance. Spend some time and be honest with yourself. If you're unsure how you handle stress, talk to your partner about their experience and gain insight from each other. You can use the questions below as a starting point.

Think about a time when you've been really weighed down by several stressors simultaneously.

- Are you adept at recognizing and expressing your emotional experiences?

- Do you shy away from sharing your emotional experiences, get overwhelmed and shut down easily, and struggle to identify more than a few basic feelings?

- Do you snap into gear and start chipping away the pieces to solve the problem?

- Do you feel frozen and struggle to get out of bed?

- Do you get disorganized, quiet, or irritable?

- Can you manage quite a lot, or do you get flustered at the first sign of trouble?

None of these reactions is bad—they are simply natural survival strategies that serve a purpose. Try not to be hard on yourself if you feel you don't handle stress well. You're looking for opportunities to acknowledge your tendencies as they are so you can move forward. If you know you struggle with remaining patient the thirteenth time you tuck a child into bed or when you get an eye roll from the teen in your life, you know where to take extra deep breaths to set yourself up for success so you can respond appropriately.

RECOGNIZING YOUR CONCERNS

The second factor is to understand your concerns. As the biological parent, what are you worried about in regard to your children? Are you worried about how your children will get along with your new partner? Maybe you have concerns about whether your children are cared for properly at their other home, or how your children will adjust to their new normal. You might also have concerns about co-parenting with your new partner or worries about how your partner might handle the stress of being a stepparent.

As a stepparent, what concerns are you bringing into this? You might have worries over whether your stepchildren will like you, how you will co-parent with your new partner, and how the other biological parent will relate with you. You may have heard war stories or tales of success from other stepparents, and you may be nervous about where your experience will fit in. Do you worry that you might struggle in your relationship with your partner?

UNDERSTANDING ACCEPTANCE

Acceptance is not being *okay* with something. There are plenty of things in life you'll need to accept that you'll never feel okay about. Acceptance is a *willingness* to see the way your life truly is. You know you've drifted out of acceptance when you land in aversion or attachment. Aversion is not wanting what you have, whereas attachment is wanting what you can't have.

Here's an example:

- Acceptance says, "Sometimes I don't feel as connected and patient with my stepkids as I do my own."

- Aversion says, "I hate how I'm always frustrated with my stepkids. Why does dealing with them have to be so hard?"

- Attachment says, "I wish my stepkids would just be easier to deal with, more like my kids."

Though the words don't differ all that much, the emotional experience of these thoughts are quite different. Notice how heavy and tense aversion and attachment are, whereas acceptance feels lighter and more open.

You might have worries about whether your family will have an in-group/out-group dynamic. Often when parts of a family were together before, they can carry a biological in-group mentality that can leave a stepparent confused, frustrated, and lonely. In the beginning of your family forming there may be people who feel like insiders and outsiders. Sometimes those roles will feel stuck, even to the insiders. If you try to force this dynamic to change, sometimes the children can end up feeling like the outsiders. What worries do you feel you have about whether this dynamic will happen in your home? What are some ways you might plan ahead to minimize the effects of this dynamic?

These are all normal concerns that could be in the back of your mind. When you bring them into your awareness, they'll be less likely to unintentionally influence your decisions, words, and actions. Pay attention to what makes you particularly anxious and plan extra self-care around these times. This will help you make the best choices for your family moving forward.

RECOGNIZING YOUR FEARS

Third, what fears do you have about how your children will react to the new family? Both biological parents and stepparents may have fears about how the children will fare. Will they be open to new stepparents, siblings, and extended family? Maybe you fear they'll struggle and not say anything. Or perhaps you're worried about the opposite—that they'll explode over difficult feelings. It is important that all parents acknowledge their fears and feelings for the children in their homes. This means being honest with yourself about what you're afraid will happen and communicating about it with your partner. You might also need to let your children know your fears. This can be used in a conversation with kids about their own fears: "Our situation's tough—I've had some fears about our family coming together, too." Use these opportunities to empathize and normalize your children's experiences.

How you feel about children impacts how you relate to them. Whatever your feelings, concerns, or fears, they're normal. Fear is your brain's way of trying to keep you alive. Though fear and anxiety don't always feel productive, remember that your brain is on your side when you're worrying. Being aware of and communicating about the way you feel will help ensure you don't make significant parenting decisions based on your fear. Use the relationship you have with your partner to sort through these thoughts. Maybe your partner has had the same fear. Or perhaps they can help support you in problem solving or reassuring you that you can figure things out together. If you find yourself unable to sleep, are more irritable, or are struggling to focus at work for more than a week or two, you may want to reach out to a counselor for additional support. Counselors are quite accessible for the majority of the U.S. population. Insurance often covers mental health services, and many insurance companies will even cover telehealth for those living in rural communities. Some local mental health centers and counseling co-ops offer sliding scale services as well.

Find Your Parenting Boundaries

Each family unit has gotten used to how they move around one another in their original setup. They have shared expectations about time together, space, and communication. You might find that one family loves talking about emotions whereas the other prefers to deal with things on their own. Or perhaps one family will be more physically affectionate, whereas another prefers to keep to themselves. Boundaries help us navigate these issues, and guide what limits, house rules, and expectations we have. I think of the terms *boundaries* and *limits* as interchangeable when related to parenting interventions.

Let's look at our expectations and the grace the children will need as you begin to parent as a unit. Will you go easier on them for a while? Will you maintain course with the boundaries they are used to? How will you introduce new boundaries and set family expectations?

You've started to understand how to communicate clearly and effectively with your partner, as well as to acknowledge your own feelings and experiences so they don't unnecessarily color your decisions and parenting. As you begin to talk about boundaries, writing down your instincts and priorities beforehand may help, so you can compare notes and work together. You should both plan on dropping some of your own initial list items and adopting some of your partner's—this is about compromise. Your expectations and values are based on the values your family had in place when you were growing up. While engaging in conversations about how your new family will determine boundaries, keep in mind what values are underlying your list. Your expectations will need to adjust over time as you learn more about your family.

For example, most of my boundaries are regarding my value of safety. In the home, there is no running, climbing to unsafe heights, or throwing objects as engaging in these kinds of behaviors is unsafe for everyone. In other homes, the free movement of children is paramount. Whatever your values, you must have reasons for being uncomfortable with certain behaviors. Kids are excellent investigators, and they're going to want to know the why behind a limit. "Because I said so," is not an answer that elicits respect. "Because I am worried for your safety," "Because we need to be respectful of one another and our home," and "Because when you get so worked up, you often get overwhelmed and upset" are better answers. Be prepared to have more *whys* underneath those answers, too. To do this, you must first understand your feelings, concerns, and fears. You'll be better able to communicate them clearly, and in so doing your children will be more likely to respect your boundaries.

Boundaries are necessary in raising children. They communicate what is allowable, appropriate, and appreciated. Well-placed boundaries help provide children with stability, encourage resiliency, and teach responsibility. Aim to choose and enforce boundaries with a long-term reason in mind: You want your children to be able to maintain friendships, hold down a job, or take care of themselves and manage stress as they grow.

SETTING LIMITS

If you're afraid for your kids, you might overcompensate and be too lenient or strict. Though these reactions come with the best intentions—to support and lessen the burden of change for your kids—they're not always helpful. Children do best when they can have their feelings and know that you will remain consistent in your affection and structure. Sometimes in blending families, you might want to give your kids a little more room for testing limits. That's okay to do, but do so intentionally. Don't always say, "Well it's a transition day," to excuse disrespect. Kids quickly learn whether they get too much space, and they push back on this space with the hope that they'll find a boundary. *Boundaries help kids feel safe.* Instead of making excuses for them, lean in and get curious about their experiences. Then let them know when you're going to start tightening the expectations again.

When limits are inappropriately set, they can do more harm than good. If you say, "You may not . . . ," you must follow through, or be willing to go back and say, "I was wrong when I said that, and here's why." If you say no and allow children to do those things anyway, they start to feel unsafe and often act out. Children want boundaries that are consistent, reliable, and trustworthy. If you are unsure, say, "Let me think about that," or, "I'm not sure how I feel." Take some time and reapproach later. Don't leave those conversations hanging. Better to not set a boundary than to set one with which you won't follow through. This will save you a headache in the long run, as well, because each time you give in to a previously set boundary, you'll have to set that limit another 10 times before your children will begin to believe that you mean what you say. Get ahead of the game by being judicious with your word.

Additionally, try asking for what you want with kids instead of correcting what you don't want. For example, if a teenager is about to run out of the house, say to them, "I'd like you to stay home," instead of, "Don't you walk out that door." When upset, kids hear only part of what you are saying. In the first example, they hear, "stay home." In the second, they hear, "walk out that door." Can you feel the difference between the two? A notable factor is your body language and tone of voice. Keep your voice low and firm and resist the urge to give back any attitude your child might be giving you. Model what you want from them. If you expect to be spoken to with respect, show them what that feels like. Pay attention to your body language, as well. Are you facing them head-on? Or are you giving them some space and turning to the side? Be aware if you slink away from their boundary testing. Remind yourself they *want* you to be their parent, so stand confidently in that role, while also remaining flexible and open. Give yourself grace if you find this to be a struggle. Skills are built over time.

Your Biological Children

Your biological children are adjusting to having a new family because of your decision to be in this new relationship. How does knowing this impact your parenting? Some may feel anxiety or guilt, whereas others, pride and excitement. Perhaps you feel a mix of emotions. Whatever your experience, support the process by acknowledging your feelings about how this new family is impacting your children.

Children are often afraid of losing importance with their biological parents. When new families move in, they can feel replaced or set aside. Imagine your home has always been a certain way: pictures of you and your family, a room that's all yours, your belongings throughout the house. You belong. Then imagine someone moves in, replaces your pictures with theirs, moves belongings around, and sets yours aside. Suddenly your home stops feeling like your home. With your stuff gone, where do *you* belong? I went through this when my dad remarried. I had a new, adorable little stepbrother who suddenly got my bunk bed, my stuffed animals, and my room. As an adult I understand why: I wasn't at my dad's as often as my little brother was. He lived there all the time. I was getting older, so I didn't need my childhood things anymore. But as a young person, I was terrified my dad didn't love me as much as he loved his new family. I've had to be careful of this in my home with my children now, too. I can feel the urge to push aside unused items that belong to my stepdaughter. Sometimes I even notice I have more patience for my daughter's unused items than I have for my stepdaughter's. I check myself often and recall the feelings of my youth to try to carve out space that remains just hers, even when those spaces sit with untouched old toys. We'll deal with them as she's ready.

Your children will need your conscious effort to remind them that they belong with you, no matter who else lives in your home. Remind them often of your feelings for them. If those feelings ever get distant with the daily grind, remember your experience when you first met them. Those tiny fingers, that heavenly baby smell, those adorable locks. Conjure up the feeling you had when you first held them in your arms. You loved them more than seemed possible and wanted the world for them. Imagining this, can you feel the warmth in your chest? Interact with your children with this warmth, whether you're appreciating their art or asking them to get in the car for the sixth time.

A note here about families whose children came into their lives in other ways, such as through adoption. These skills and plans will all still apply—you just entered your child's life in a different way. They'll still look to you for support and love. They'll still want to know you see them and want them. This might be intensified with adopted children, as their brains know some abandonment fear and require more regulation from you to stay balanced.

Parents, you have some things you'll need to consider and talk about with your partner:

- How will you make parenting fair between all kids?

- Will you be giving your children special consideration and extra grace as they adjust?

- How does your partner feel about that grace period?

- What do you think your responsibility is in helping the children adjust?

- What are some cherished rituals you can keep just for you and your kids?

How your children feel about the transitions they are going through may impact your relationship with them, and you will need to talk this through with them in age-appropriate ways:

- How do your children feel about their new family members?

- How is their relationship with your new partner?

- What might help them feel connected to you?

- What do they hope will stay the same? Or change?

- What are they worried about? Excited about?

Get curious about their experiences and respect them. Your children might have completely different beliefs and emotions about the experience of bringing this family together than you do. Go into these conversations, as much as possible, without assumptions and be willing to hear hard truths. You'll need to share some of this feedback with your partner, but for other feelings, you may just need to empathize in the moment. For example, if your child is telling you that something your partner is doing is hurting their feelings, and it's something that's changeable like the way your partner greets your children in the morning, that would be worth sharing with your partner. However, if what is bothering them is unchangeable, like not wanting a new family at all, that may not be necessary to share. Keep your children's confidence when appropriate, but involve your partner when doing so would help relationships grow. You might tell the children you'll talk to your partner about issues, encourage older children to do so on their own or with you present, or offer your partner hints to improve their relationship privately. When in doubt, ask the children what they'd prefer to have happen.

Your children will need to receive the consistent message that you love them, hear them out, and expect respect from them. Send the clear and consistent message that they belong with you, unconditionally. They need to know, also, that you feel the same way about the other members of your family. You want your children to feel everyone in the family is equally valued. You want your children to feel they are not more important, and not less. This equality helps foster trust and respect in the family unit.

Pay special attention to ways you can maintain your connection with your children. In my practice, I often hear children expressing sadness about their biological parent choosing a new partner over the children. With their natural uncertainty and fears, your children will be more likely to experience a sense of separateness as their family changes, especially if a new baby is brought into the picture. Though the relationship with your partner will be paramount in order to help the family stay strong, your relationship with your children will need reassurance. Look for ways to keep dedicated, special times just between the two of you. If you have a Sunday morning cartoon and banana smoothie ritual, keep it as a time for just you and your kids. Let your children be the ones to invite your partner, in their own time. Maintaining these shared moments helps ease some of the worry children might otherwise face.

Additionally, supporting your children's relationship with their new stepparent will help streamline the transition. Your job will be to listen to your children's concerns and help them process and work through what might be helpful to improve those relationships. Though you'll need to make clear that your new partner is here to stay, you'll also need to balance that with *not agreeing* with your children about the things with which they're struggling. For instance, if your child says to you, "She is so rude! I didn't even do anything," you don't want to agree with them by saying, "I know, she can be pretty rude sometimes." You want to empathize with them: "Sometimes what she says feels rude to you, and you're not sure what you're doing wrong. That's tough." Follow up with thought-provoking questions like, "What is an example of that, maybe I can help?" or, "What might we be able to do to clear the air?" or, "Why do you think she said those things?"

Listen with the intention of empathizing with and understanding your children. Depending on their age, see if they can take any responsibility in those interactions. Then, talk to your partner at a later time in private. Help your partner understand how the children are feeling and brainstorm ways to improve the relationship. Facilitating a family meeting where the children can express themselves and feel heard might help. Emphasize communication. You might need to help by being an intermediary between your partner and your children at first, but work toward having them learning how to talk things through on their own.

You will always have a special bond with your children. Honor and nurture that relationship to help keep the family strong. As the biological parent, you have the most responsibility in this new family. You will need to care for the relationships you have with your new partner, your biological children, and any stepchildren. Each relationship will need your presence of mind, intention, and appreciation to prevent resentment and jealousy. As each person feels seen, accepted, and loved by you, and understands their equal importance in your life, they will be better able to share a healthy relationship with one another.

Your Stepchildren

Being a stepparent is harder than being a biological parent. There, the hard truth has been said. As difficult as stepparenting might be, though, it is a worthwhile job. Great stepparents are those who show up as themselves, prioritize the emotions and needs of their stepkids, and respect the various roles and relationships in the family. Let's look at what steps to take to improve your stepparenting relationships.

The best way to describe the proper role of a stepparent is to be like an aunt or an uncle. When aunts and uncles are around, they might set a limit or two, but they defer to the parent for significant discipline, which I'll talk about in its own section in this chapter (see pages 70–74). Sometimes they act as a confidant, babysitter, or cheerleader. Ultimately, they care deeply for their nieces and nephews but don't automatically assume full responsibility for them. They can make suggestions, but they acknowledge that the big decisions are up to their parents. Their love has some respectful distance, ensuring that children aren't confused about what this adult's role is.

There isn't one perfect way to be a stepparent, but there are plenty of fun, creative, and caring ways to be a great one. As a stepparent, you'll need to find your own identity. You may be more like a biological parent, especially when the child's other biological parent is absent or has died. You may be more like a distant aunt or uncle, stepping in only when the family is doing something fun together. Part of your identity will be your own, the other part will come from how your partner and stepchildren see your role in their lives. For a smooth adjustment, talk about these expectations with your partner and children to find what works best for you as well as them.

Many stepparents will get to a place where they feel they truly love their stepchildren as they do their biological ones. Some will love their stepchildren in a different way than their biological kids, and still others will never feel like they love their stepchildren. What matters more than loving your stepchildren is respecting and caring for them. Just as you cannot force a family to feel like a family, you cannot force love that doesn't develop naturally. This doesn't mean the relationship is doomed; rather the relationship simply has a different tone. Be open with yourself about how you feel and allow space for everyone in the family to do the same.

Just as you may or may not develop love for your stepchildren, your stepchildren may or may not develop love for you, in return. You have these beautiful children in your life whom you laugh with, enjoy, worry over, and care for. Their lives are entwined with and impact yours. And yet, you will not necessarily get the natural benefits of raising children. In most relationships, after there is a rupture—like an argument, a broken promise, or mean words—a repair is made. Between children and their parents, this repair typically happens with story time at night, saying sorry and hugging, or kids later offering to help. This is children's way of mending a relationship and reconnecting. This doesn't always happen in stepparent relationships, so your responsibility will become to manage that experience and do your own repairs.

This is one of the hardest parts of being a stepparent. In any other relationship, if there were repeated ruptures without repair, you would no longer engage in that relationship. With your stepchildren, you must find a way to forgive and mend to keep that relationship healthy and moving forward. Dealing with a child who is acting out can be harder when you don't feel responsible for their discipline. Relying on your partner for help is important so that you feel included and respected. Over time, as you build trust and have positive interactions, your relationship with your stepchildren can get to a place where everything feels easier.

Keep your focus on what you appreciate about your stepchildren and choose to see the next time they engage with you in a positive way as their attempt at repairing the relationship, even if you don't believe that's their intention. Work to see them with unconditional positive regard so your behavior toward them is supportive of a strong relationship. I highly recommend that stepparents find a community with people who understand their experience: other stepparents, friends, their partner, family, or a counselor who specializes in blending families. Create a tribe for yourself to normalize your experiences, give you ideas for ways of increasing connection between you and your stepkids, and reduce your stress. One way you might increase connection with your stepchildren is to get curious about what they're interested in. Have them teach you about their interest or take them to see something they're excited about. Show that you care about their interests and opinions.

You'll want to lean on your partner as you discover this new role in your life. Talk to them. A stepparent feeling like an outsider in the family at first is pretty normal. For some families, there will always be a slight in-group/out-group dynamic. You won't get the same experience with your partner that you may have experienced in the past in relationships without children. Especially for stepparents who don't have their own children, it can be a strange adjustment of expectations. Parents are used to having a child around. You are not. Notice any signs of jealousy or feelings of being left out and try to pluck these thoughts before they take root. Remind yourself that you chose to live with a *family*.

Parenting Together

You know that you have different relationships with your biological children than with your stepchildren. Regardless of the relationship, rules and discipline need to be as equal as possible for all the children in the home. As a couple, showing a united front to the children regarding house rules, expectations, and discipline is necessary for success. One of the biggest mistakes I see couples make—and one of the biggest mistakes I made early on—is losing sight of who sets rules and who follows through with discipline, especially in the beginning. I'll be describing techniques, approaches, and perspectives to consider as you journey down this path. Keep communication as a couple in the front of your mind. Strive to remain open, compassionate, considerate, and conscientious to find a compromise that will bring your family together.

RULES

Imagine working a job your entire life under a specific boss. You may not appreciate every aspect of their management style, but over the years you become accustomed to the way they do things. Then one day, they come in and say they've decided to hire a new manager who has completely different ideas for your job. Your original boss, trying to help ease the transition and keep the new manager around, goes along with many of the new ideas and rules the new manager brings. The confusion, frustration, and exhaustion you might feel trying to navigate the new parameters, wondering where (and whether) you'll fit in long-term . . . phew!

And you're an *adult*.

Thankfully, kids have the potential to be much more adaptable than grown-ups sometimes feel they themselves are. Keeping this in mind, let's talk about rules. If the rules stay the same as the biological parent has always done them, then the stepparent's resentment, confusion, and frustration can build. What about their parenting values? Their boundaries? Their comfort levels? Having someone, child or not, living in your home in a way that doesn't align with your values is difficult. This gets infinitely more complicated when a new baby comes into the picture. The stepparent is not necessarily going to want to parent the way their partner decided to before blending the family. Nor can the stepparent's way of parenting be the only way. You want to parent together.

To begin, create rules as a couple at a time when the children are not present, and not currently testing those rules. Some expectations might be easy, making agreement effortless. Some may be more complicated as your upbringings and family cultures collide. Try prioritizing expectations that mean the most to you and compare notes with your partner. Make a game of it! Both of you write down your natural response to various parenting issues that may arise. Count to three and share your answers. Talk to each other about the *why* behind those answers. What value are you trying to teach in that moment? Then look for solutions and family expectations that meet both parents' wishes. If you get stuck, put that example aside and come back to it another time. Keep the conversation positive and productive. These exercises are meant to bring you closer as a couple, not drive you apart.

THE *DOS* AND *DON'TS* OF BEING A NEW STEPPARENT

DO: Approach your relationship as an amazing aunt or uncle. You are in a supportive role.

DON'T: Try to make your stepchildren feel like *your* children. If this type of relationship happens—great, but don't get hung up on worrying that you ought to feel like they are yours.

DO: Work toward improving the connection with your stepchildren. Take them on special dates, bring them a trinket from your travels, engage them in games, or check in with them on how they're doing regularly. Try to have fun and see them with an unconditional positive regard.

DON'T: Pressure yourself to love your stepchildren. Some stepparents love their stepchildren, and some don't. What matters more is respect, care, and appreciation.

DO: Trust your partner to take care of the heavy lifting with parenting. Focus your energy on building a positive relationship, including trust, fun, and consistency with your stepkids.

DON'T: Set boundaries before you have a solid, respectful, positive relationship.

DO: Reach out for support from other people who know what you're going through. This can be friends, family, or a counselor.

DON'T: Get stuck in feeling like a stepparent island. You are not alone.

Keep in mind you are creating rules for *your home*. If you have a great relationship with your ex, you may be able to create consistency between your children's homes. You get bonus points if you all sit down together, biological parents and stepparents, to discuss them! If not, you still must present consistent expectations for your home. Over time, the kids will learn to adjust to different rules in different homes. You cannot make (or hold back from making) rules in your home based on what other people do in their homes. You can only know your values and live within them to the best of your ability.

Once the rules have been agreed upon, the child's biological parent introduces them slowly. Prioritize the rules based on what is most important to you and your partner. Build on them over time, starting with one or two easy ones and working up from there. If you have older kids, ask for their input on the rules. They might have great ideas. Bring those ideas back to the table with your partner—don't just agree to them on the spot. You're a united front, remember?

Whether the stepparent is present when discussing rules with the children will depend on your family, your children, and the relationships that are already in place. Trust your instincts. As the biological parent, communicate the need for respect of the rules and of all the adults in the home. Explain that when you aren't present, their stepparent will be the one who enforces the rules. They are not a tattletale; they are helping the family come together openly and honestly. *You are a team.*

HERE'S A TOOL TO HELP YOU
SET LIMITS AND KEEP THE PEACE:

- **P**ause. The goal is to respond, not react. Create space between feeling upset and executing a limit. Try starting with a deep breath.

- **E**mpathize with their emotion or motivation. Before setting the limit, help them feel understood. "I know you're upset because you wanted today to be just us. . . ."

- **A**pply the limit. This is where you communicate the limit. Keep it short, and try using "and" after empathizing, as "but" often undoes what comes before it: ". . . and it isn't okay to yell at your siblings."

- **C**onsider alternatives. For older children, pose a question: "What else can you do?" For younger children, you might need to give an option or two: "You can come tell me you're disappointed, take a deep breath, or ask for time just for us."

- **E**xpect growth, not perfection. Help them look for opportunities to make circumstances easier next time. "What might help you feel better before getting to the point of yelling again?" or "What did that feel like in your body? What can we do next time you feel that coming?" There will be more opportunities for them to practice. Learning takes repetition.

DISCIPLINE

For our purposes here, discipline is the set of expectations you set for your children, and the consequences you use to communicate to them when their behavior is inappropriate for your family's values. Notice we will not be using the word *punishment* interchangeably with *discipline*. Punishment is a harsh consequence that is unrelated to the offending behavior. For example, time-outs. If a child throws a toy in frustration, a punishment is removing them from social contact for a short amount of time. Most often with punishment, children don't learn what we've intended. We think they're sitting there "thinking about what they did," when really, they're sitting there thinking we're mean and that they can't rely on our support when they're struggling with emotion. This isn't supporting our connection with them.

Alternatively, natural consequences help children understand cause and effect. If I throw this toy, I lose the privilege of playing with this toy for a short time. For little kids, think mere minutes. For older kids, think hours. You can also have children earn privileges back. If they do something to take away from the family, they must do something to give back to the family. Included in the concept of discipline is the emotional attunement necessary to communicate why a *behavior* is unacceptable. Children are always accepted, but not all behavior is. When children struggle with emotions and behavior, our job is to turn toward them and help them figure out more helpful ways to manage feelings. In discussing discipline, remember these parts: expectations, consequences, and emotional attunement.

When our beloved children go through complete upheaval, uncertainty, and loss, we naturally want to protect them. You may feel for them, want to give them space to process, and defend them, including their not-so-great behavior, to anyone who suggests otherwise. As difficult as the transition is and as hard as putting boundaries in place can feel when kids are already struggling, children need consistent expectations to feel safe.

Just as you sat down to create the rules, so will you decide on the discipline in the home. In the beginning, all discipline should be done by the children's biological parent. Though the stepparent can enforce rules when the biological parent is not home, any consequences attached should come from the biological parent later. This is vital until the children and stepparents create a trusting, respectful relationship. Plan on this taking a year or two of positive interactions. Over time, once the stepparent has a solid, positive relationship with the kids, they can begin to intervene with discipline, especially on day-to-day tasks. These day-to-day tasks might look like ensuring they do their chores and homework before they play video games or go to a friend's house. You could ask them to set the table for dinner or put away their belongings, and set limits around unsafe behavior or pre-established house rules.

Use open communication channels to keep assessing how the relationships are going. You want to balance giving the children space to allow a healthy relationship with their stepparent to grow, while not making the stepparent feel powerless if the children act up or are disrespectful. If you find the kids are struggling to remain respectful or are taking advantage of the stepparent, the time has come to hand over the power of the day-to-day discipline when the biological parent isn't home. Have the biological parent make that clear to the children. Ultimately, you're trying to avoid any potential adversarial relationships, which can be difficult to heal. Most people take direction better from managers they trust and respect than from those of whom they think little.

If you already find yourself in one of these adversarial relationships, take a step back. This negative dynamic can result when the biological parent is the more relaxed parent naturally and continues to be relaxed with the addition of the new stepparent. The new stepparent either is naturally stricter or senses the need for more boundaries and sets them before the children are emotionally prepared to receive them. Discipline only works when mutual respect is present. If you're stuck, take some deep breaths and focus more of your energy on the relationship with your stepchildren and less on making sure they follow the rules. Engage your partner in more discussions around what boundaries you find you need to feel comfortable. The adults in the home need to work together to improve relationships—stepparents alone cannot improve a situation they see needing to be fixed.

As the biological parent, you cannot continue to parent the way you used to. Whether you were previously the fun parent or the strict parent, you must blend those two in this new dynamic. To support your new partner's relationship with your children, you need to step up the discipline. When the children are in your care, you have full responsibility for them. Your partner is there to support you, not to parent your children. You will be the model of respect in the house. You're also the model of love, laughter, and relaxing into these new roles. You can do this.

DECISIONS

Similar to rules and discipline, decisions should remain the responsibility of the biological parents. In most places, legally, large-scale decision-making is shared between parents unless there is a court order specifying otherwise. These types of decisions include the school the children attend, the activities they join, the religion they follow, and which doctors they see.

This part can be hard for stepparents, because you're living with children you care for, worry about, and have in your daily life. And yet, you don't get to call any of the shots. Not only that, but those shots will impact your life in various ways. What school a child goes to or the activities they join make a difference in your family's finances, schedule, and living arrangements. Although potentially frustrating, respecting the relationships that were present before you and your partner began blending the family is vital. You're respecting the biological parents by trusting they know what's best for their children. You're respecting the children by not assuming that you, who may not have known them as deeply or as long, know better than their parents what is best for them.

This doesn't mean stepparents should have no influence. Biological parents can respect their new partners by bringing them in to their half of the conversation. You can have discussions in your home about possible decisions and decide together on behalf of your family. Ultimately, though, if you disagree, the decision should be left up to the biological parent. Even if you agree, together you are only half the equation.

If your family has an absent other parent and you wish to share decisions with your partner, please do so, but judiciously. With younger children, the adjustment can go fairly smoothly as they're still forming their own opinions. Older children and teenagers, though, may need you to bring stepparent influence in slowly over time, offering it as an option, not a requirement. If the children ask for a stepparent's opinion on major decisions, all the better. After all, most people prefer to get advice only when they ask for it.

When relationships with ex-spouses are particularly difficult, these decisions can get messy quickly. Keep your focus on what's best for your family, your relationships, and your children. There are ways to solve disputes, including the use of mediation or parental coordinators. You may also reach out to counselors to help all of you learn to communicate and work together for the betterment of your children's lives.

KEY POINTS IN PARENTING TOGETHER

- You are a team. Strive to be a united front. Communicate about expectations and experiences when the children aren't around to problem solve on your own.

- Accept each other's influence in the way you approach and parent all children in the home. Acknowledge that you both bring something positive to the team, and you both still have things to learn.

- The biological parent retains 100% of their parenting responsibility. Stepparents are there in a supportive role and can help when appropriate for the relationship they have with the children. Biological parents present the rules, discipline, and decisions.

- Give relationships with your partner's children time to build, and time to heal if they've struggled. Relationships and repairs happen over long periods of time—plan on two years before the new relationship feels natural and the old one has faded away.

- Your family is unique and will require ongoing effort to explore, define, and develop over time. You have a great opportunity to make the dynamic as you want.

- Remember that you are not alone. If you're struggling to integrate your family, reach out for support and find others who understand and can help guide you.

Co-Parenting with Ex-Spouse(s)

Whatever the structure of your home life with your blended family might be, you could be facing any number of situations with ex-spouses. You and your current partner may both have been married, just one of you, or neither of you. You may have more than one ex-spouse you share kids with, and your ex-spouses could have new partners of their own. Learning how to co-parent with all these adults can seem overwhelming. If the co-parenting doesn't go smoothly for everyone, don't give up hope just yet. You never know how life can change as the kids grow older and their parents wiser. If you're still forming your co-parenting relationship or already have the beginnings of a great one, even if your relationship is strained, let's turn now to how to work together.

WORKING WITH EX-SPOUSES

The key to relationships with ex-spouses is the same as with your current partner: communication. The communication will, of course, take on a different tone than the communication you have with your current partner. Think of your relationship with your ex-spouse as a business relationship. You are in the business of raising your children to be wonderful, successful, happy adults. All the adults in the situation must put their own hurt feelings, agendas, and pasts aside.

In business relationships, you hold yourself to a higher standard than you do in personal relationships. You consider how you engage with someone to be sure you are being respectful, helpful, and effective. You keep your eye on the work at hand without getting caught up in personal vendettas. You even alter your voice when answering the phone, to portray a positive, helpful tone. Business relationships try to be flexible to serve the work best. Your children are the work. You want to be seen and experienced as trustworthy, approachable, reasonable, and respectful. You're also more forgiving of business partners than you might be in other relationships, because you acknowledge they are doing the best they can. When appropriate, you're comfortable offering and accepting constructive feedback. If you engage your ex in a business partnership for the betterment of your children's lives, everyone benefits.

If at all possible, plan on sitting down in person with your ex-spouse at least every six months to discuss the upbringing of your shared children. Work together to check in on how things are going—any successes and any concerns. See how the other person is handling chores, homework, and bedtimes. Look for opportunities to increase consistency and the smoothness of transitions. Go to the same parent-teacher conferences instead of scheduling separate ones. The sting of divorce and separated parents is significantly less when those parents can get along.

When parents work together to raise their children, this is called co-parenting. Again, the goal is not necessarily to be your ex's best friend, though if you can manage friendship, all the better. At minimum, strive for a polite, friendly, respectful, and collaborative business partnership.

Another type of parenting is called parallel parenting. Parallel parenting is as sounds: Two people parent separately from each other as the child switches between homes. They do not work together or interact. They have separate parent-teacher meetings, birthday parties, and if there is any communication, a service—like the online chat system Talking Parents—can keep some distance between them. If your relationship with your ex-spouse is particularly difficult, uncooperative, or unsafe, parallel parenting might be the best option for you.

Children ultimately need at least one positive, secure attachment to be healthy. This means that if you can be attuned and responsive to their needs and bids for connection, that is enough. Remember this if your children are unable to engage in a relationship with their other biological parent due to that parent's death, incarceration, or any other reason for absence. Having both biological parents in the children's lives won't always be possible or advisable in cases of abuse, for instance. In these situations, the children's attachment and safety with you, their primary caregiver, become all-important. This includes families who have children through adoption. Again, children can create new, secure attachments, and they just need one. You can be enough.

Keeping the issues in the relationship separate from the issues of parenting can be a challenge. Too often, parents bad-mouth or belittle their ex to their children. They may make comments in passing like, "Your mom should be taking better care of you," or, "Of course your father forgot to bring what you need." They might also insinuate that the relationship with the other parent is poor, like, "Are they being nice to you?" and, "I'm sorry you have to go to their home." In more extreme cases, they may refuse to have pictures of the other parent in their home, throw out correspondence, withhold the child, or share adult information with them. In fact, all of these are examples of what is called parental alienation, which is very serious, so serious that some places are beginning to recognize these acts of alienation as emotional child abuse. This can feel extreme when you're just frustrated with the way things are going, I know. But realizing just how serious this behavior is to children's brains is crucial. Kids, especially those who are younger, look to their parents for guidance. They're not fully independent thinkers and are easily swayed. If a child is uncertain, worried you will withdraw your love, or scared, they will often go along with anything you say. As a parent, you have the ultimate power. Use your power gently so they have the freedom to make up their own minds.

No matter how you feel about your ex, no matter what they did in the relationship they had with you, *that person is your baby's parent*. You want to give the world to your children, so why not give them the gift of a great relationship with all their parents? This gift means more than you can see from the vantage point of anger and disappointment. Offering your child an opportunity to have a positive relationship with all involved parents helps their brains develop in ways that lead them to be successful, confident, secure adults. To grow into healthy adults, children need to know and experience love from those who raise

"Your children will need your conscious effort to remind them that they belong with you, no matter who else lives in your home."

them. If that includes both biological parents, encouraging them to have positive relationships is helpful for their well-being.

This also means encouraging your children to have positive relationships with your ex's new partner. How the new partner came into the picture doesn't matter. *What is important is that you give your children explicit permission to like their stepfamilies.* The children are the primary people harmed when parents try to position their children against their stepparents. Allowing your children to enjoy their stepfamilies can be difficult when there was cheating involved, if you feel jealous, or if you simply don't like your ex's new partner. Over and over, I will encourage you to consider your kids. What is in their best interest? Would you rather your children feel hatred, act out, and isolate themselves? Or would you rather your children find another awesome adult relationship where they are cared for, encouraged, and supported? What does each approach teach them about love, family, and respect?

If your children express disliking their stepparent on the other side, you can listen to them, empathize, and maybe even encourage them to talk to their other parent. Imperative, however: Stick to three points. First, do not agree with the negative statements they make about their stepparents, *even if you agree on the inside.* Second, tell them explicitly that you want them to have a positive relationship and that they have some age-appropriate responsibility to make an effort. This might simply be an encouragement not to ignite fights, but instead to walk away or ask for help. Third, encourage respect in the face of a difficult relationship. The quickest way to gain respect is to offer it.

If you find these tasks difficult or insurmountable, there are resources out there for you to get extra support. Look for a local counselor who specializes in blending families. If you can't get all parties to engage, you can at least have a safe place to explore your feelings, process what triggers you, and look for ways to better manage your side of the situation. There are also structured classes to help facilitate co-parenting with ex-spouses. You can check with your local mental health center or justice center, library, or community school for recommendations.

YOUR PARTNER'S EX-SPOUSE

As you focus on building a united front with your new partner, you may also need to navigate relationships with any of your partner's ex-spouses when you share parenting responsibilities. How will you factor into one another's parenting plans, or will you? If you can have a productive relationship with your partner's ex-spouse in regard to co-parenting, there are some things to keep in mind to increase the efficacy of these relationships.

If you are new to the picture or are trying to refresh your relationship with your partner's ex-spouse, see if you can spend some alone time with them. When stepparents and ex-spouses are able to meet one another over coffee, happy hour, or a game of putt-putt, they're better able to create a relationship with which the children can feel good. Spending time with the other biological parent can also help that parent understand and feel more comfortable with who is spending time with their children. People can build others up in their minds as more callous and conniving than they are, and getting to know them is a great way to diffuse some of that negative energy. You can also have kid-dates with them and go to arcades, painting classes, or book readings at the library. Spending time with your partner's ex-spouse shows your kids that you prioritize and care for them. It also shows that they can make the best of a situation and that they don't need to live with the tension of a family who refuses to work together. The relationship you form with your partner's ex-spouse doesn't have to be friendship, but can be acquaintanceship. This is a powerful stance to take.

Though this is the ideal, having such an acquaintanceship won't be possible for every family. Do what feels possible for your circumstances. Stretch yourself emotionally until you're uncomfortable, because this means you are growing, but if you're experiencing pain, pull back. If your spouse's ex-partner is particularly uncooperative, perhaps the best way for you to improve your relationship with them is to remain respectful and courteous.

There are two key points in making that relationship with your partner's ex-spouse possible. The first is to respect the history of their past relationship. At some point, they liked each other enough to create children together, maybe even loved each other enough to be married. They have positive and negative experiences that happened outside your relationship. They have shared memories, special moments, and those intimate first days with their babies. Instead of feeling alienated by this, try to feel respectful toward it. Without that relationship, their children wouldn't be part of your life. As the stepparent, your job isn't to come in and fill in the gaps left by ex-spouses. Your job is to come in and be a great addition to the group.

This takes a delicate balance of confidence and respect—you need enough of both to refute any possible insecurities that may pop up. This confident respect is easier to maintain when you don't get involved in the politics of your partner's previous relationship. If your partner struggles to speak positively about their ex-spouse, or gets triggered by current behavior into past interactions, try your best to remain supportive without buying a ticket into their opinions. If their ex were completely horrible, your partner would have never been with them. Everyone has difficult aspects to their character and redeeming qualities as well. You are served best when you can empathize with your partner's struggles, while also acknowledging their ex-spouse's redeeming qualities. If you struggle to come up with these, simply recall that they helped to create the kids whose lives you get to share.

The second key point is respecting that the children love both of their parents. This is fairly easy to do when you have a positive relationship with the other biological parent. However, if you find yourself in an uncooperative relationship with the other biological parent, respecting the children's love for their other biological parent can be particularly difficult. Kids need to feel free to have their own feelings and opinions. They may or may not be receiving messages from others about how they should feel about their blended family, so keep that confident respect and try not to engage in that power struggle. Remain positive and respectful about all relationships in the family to keep your own stress levels down and to help you act in the way that aligns best with your values.

For instance, if you value honesty, you'll have to remain honest with yourself and speak truths that are necessary and kind. If you're stressed, you might exaggerate someone's negative qualities and build up anger and resentment. When you're calm, you're better able to see others for who they are, the good and the bad. Your actions are more skilled when they come from this mental place.

CHAPTER FOUR
New Family Members

Your family has more than just a few new members. Not only will there be additional parents and potentially instant siblings, your children will suddenly gain more extended stepfamily like grandparents, aunts, and cousins. You and your family will be adjusting to having not just a new in-law, but a whole new family to love. If you bring another baby into the family or if your children are already grown, there's even more to consider. Let's look at how to deal with all these new family members.

Grandparents and Step-Grandparents

Children may have grown up knowing the grandparents of their biological families. This could mean just two sets of grandparents, or more, if their parents come from blended families. Now you're adding even more by incorporating step-grandparents. In my case, my stepdaughter already had three sets: one from her dad and two from her mom. Then I came into her life, and she instantly had two more sets since my parents were divorced as well. *That's a lot of grandparents to love you.*

When you have good relationships with your parents, your kids are lucky to have these grandparents in their lives. Extended family can be good for your kids and stepkids, whether just for the beginning years or well into adulthood. At the same time, be gentle with yourself if your relationship with your parents is strained or estranged, or if your parents are no longer living. Although kids can benefit from these relationships, they can also connect with their grandparents through you. I never met my grandmother, who died when my dad was young, but I felt her presence in my life through pictures and stories of her.

As a stepparent, how close you are to your parents—both emotionally and geographically—makes a difference in how you include them. Just as you've needed time to adjust to your new family, so will your parents. The instinct can be to immediately incorporate everyone like one big happy family, but before you dive into the deep end, talk with your parents. How do they feel about having step-grandkids? What are they worried, excited, or uncertain about? How do they want to be woven into the kids' lives? You'll also want to talk to your stepkids. How do they feel about more grandparents? Have they met them already? What questions do they have? Your stepkids are already working on a lot of relationships. Step-grandparents can be an easy addition. If you face challenges, work to integrate the grandparent generation slowly to keep this connection positive.

Once you have a better understanding of how everyone feels coming together, you can bring them in as they feel comfortable. Maybe they'll want to work up to sleepovers with cousins at grandma's house. Maybe they'll always be a little emotionally distant from one another. Just like there is no perfect stepparent dynamic, there is no perfect step-grandparent one. Trust your instincts about what's possible among family members and work toward this goal slowly. Your parents will be looking to you to learn how to integrate into your stepfamily. Encourage them to include your stepchildren the way they include your biological kids.

Grandparents and step-grandparents play a valuable role in their grandchildren's lives, and also in yours. How do your parents do with your biological kids? Are they involved in every aspect of their lives? Are they distant grandparents who stay in touch through video chats? Or are they not really involved? How do your parents feel about your new relationship and immediate family? Having your parents outwardly support your relationship with your new partner can help encourage positive relationships between your partner and children, as well as your partner and your extended family. If your ex-partner was close with your family, the transition can be difficult. Sometimes the grandparents struggle to shift their loyalty, don't really understand blended family dynamics, or remain protective of you or your kids. You'll also need to make your expectations clear to your extended family. Let them know you expect respect, kindness, and consideration. Explain to them how much this new person or people mean to you. Tell your extended family about the steps the new immediate family members have already taken to begin on a positive note and discuss how your parents can help by encouraging the new relationships.

As grandparents and step-grandparents blend into your family, keep an eye on any dynamics that need to be addressed to help keep relationships supportive. Grandparents might struggle to share the attention of their grandkids with new step-grandparents or shower them with more attention and gifts in an attempt to offset the stress of the changes the children are going through. Step-grandparents might step in too quickly or not enough, or inadvertently shower their biological grandchildren with more love than they show their step-grandkids. Most of these issues are best dealt with by talking them through. Express your concerns, listen to theirs, and try to find ways to support your kids in feeling like everyone is valued. You'll need to set boundaries with both sets of grandparents to make clear what, if any, role they have in advising your parenting and blending.

Extended Family

Getting used to each other's extended families helps you feel like a solid unit. Blended families are some of the bigger families around. Not only will you have new in-laws, but you'll also still have old in-laws from ex-spouses. Your children may suddenly have a whole new host of aunts, uncles, and cousins as well. You can help your children adjust to their growing family by keeping connected to that extended family. Showing them pictures, telling them stories, and encouraging them to hang out or say hello on the phone can help children get to know and feel as though their stepfamily *is their family.*

A New Baby

A new baby can bring incredible joy into a family. The hope and excitement, those sweet, tiny baby toes. For blended families, that joy can also be met with resentment, uncertainty, and lots of tears. Though your new baby may fill your heart with love and happiness, everyone experiences things from their own perspective. For the other kids in your blended family, that new baby can mean competition. Here's what to look out for and how to respond during this transition.

AS A COUPLE

Since you, as a couple, set the tone in your family, you'll need to set the tone for how your new baby will blend into the family. The excitement of having a baby together can bring you closer as a couple.

As we've talked about in other sections of this book, you already are working on or have a system for how you handle household and parenting duties as a couple. The dynamic will change, at least temporarily, with a new baby. Pay particular attention during the first three months of your baby's life, as baby and mom will need time to get used to the rhythm of sharing their lives without sharing a body. Mom will be going through a lot of changes, within her own body and externally with her new responsibilities. Her partner will need to help with the household labor more at first to help her adjust, including helping keep the other kids engaged and bringing mom what she needs during marathon feedings. This can get tricky if mom also has other biological children. She'll want to spend time with her other children, while also feeling the pull of a newborn. Any way her partner can help support her in balancing this will bring their relationship closer. This might also be a time for her partner to get more time in with the other kids, whether they are biological children or stepchildren. If mom is not used to parenting and her partner is, then the partner might be able to help her adjust more smoothly. How have both partners been participating in parenting thus far? How might this need to change, at least at first, while everyone is adjusting? How can you use this time to shake up any parts of the family that have been otherwise stuck?

Mom isn't the only one who will be going through adjustments. Too often support systems forget to ask dads or partners how they're doing. Postpartum mood disorders, though more common in women who give birth, also occur in partners and for adoptive families. When the partner who gave birth experiences postpartum mood disorders, the other partner is more likely to experience the same. They, too, can struggle with depression, anxiety, irritability, and more. Though hormones may not play the same role in adoptive families, having a new baby in your home is still an enormous adjustment, especially if you didn't have much time to prepare for their arrival. You and your partner will be going through changes spiritually, physically, emotionally, and mentally anytime you bring a new baby into your home. Though one or both of you have done this before, you've never been through this together. As much as you'll be learning about your new baby, you'll also be learning about each other and how you handle the transition as an individual.

THE *DOS* AND *DON'TS* OF INTEGRATING EXTENDED FAMILY

DO: Encourage everyone to see your biological children, stepchildren, and shared children as equal parts of your family, and for your stepchildren to view all sides as their family, too.

DON'T: Assume all your extended family will immediately love your blended family the way you do. This process takes time.

DO: Help clarify family roles—from stepparenting to step-grandparenting—so everyone understands your approach to blending and the ways they can support *you*.

DON'T: Expect everyone to instinctively know the ways the relationships in blended families should look, sound, or act.

DO: Remain positive, open, and flexible.

DON'T: Forget to enjoy and celebrate your big new family.

Parents will need to rely on each other through this time to check in and make sure each person is getting their needs met. It can be a challenge if this is one parent's first child, as the excitement and trepidation might be heightened. First babies are different from third babies, and only in blended families do you experience partnerships where one partner may be more experienced at having kids than the other. For each of you to be at a different comfort level with babies is absolutely okay. Let first-time parents fuss and worry a little, and let seasoned parents relax and believe the kid will be fine. Listen to your partner the way you would with any other parenting venture. Even if one of you is an amateur and the other a professional, *you're still on the same team.*

AS PARENTS

As you balance how to handle your new baby as a couple, you'll also need to keep your eye on how your other kids are doing. Kids of different ages, sexes, and personalities handle these transitions in different ways. You might have one kid who loves babies and is enthralled with the new one, and another who feels jealous and won't even acknowledge their presence or will pinch them when you're not looking. Not all children follow the traditional expectations that girls will be invested in new babies while boys will show less interest. We'll talk about what to look for with different age groups, but greet your child as they are. You might anticipate they'll struggle, yet they end up as happy as can be, or vice versa. The following information provides a guide to what you might see, but you will always be the expert in what your individual children feel and need.

UNDERSTANDING CHILDREN'S RESPONSES

Very young children often adjust to this change fairly smoothly. Kids under three are at a stage that makes developing a friendship with their new sibling a natural process. They may have age-appropriate struggles like jealousy, regression, and clingy behavior, but this is often more in alignment with what first-time families would experience. Make sure to still give them physical affection, spend special time with them, and continue your regular routine. Show them how having a new sibling adds to their life.

Children between 4 and 10 may experience a higher level of jealousy or a sense of competition. At this age, children are more imaginative, aware, and have a knack for fairness. They're young enough to crave attention from their parents and old enough to realize their parents' time is a commodity. They're also better able to vocalize their discontent and might push away things that are too "babyish" as they strive for independence and autonomy. One key approach I've found working with this age group is to give them credit for how smart they are. I do my best to talk to children with my adult voice and approach them with the assumption that they are capable, curious, and involved. When you nix the baby talk and engage them in a genuine way, they're more likely to share their feelings and believe you when you say how much you still care about them. When they feel like you see them as capable young beings, you help them see themselves in this positive light. They, in turn, are better able to take responsibility for themselves, advocate for what they need, and communicate their struggles. You never know, your older children might just show up as rock star big brothers and sisters.

IDEAS FOR KEEPING SIBLINGS ENGAGED AFTER BABY COMES HOME

- Stories about siblings coming together and being a big sister or brother can help prepare kids for the transition. Get some books from your library to help open up conversations and air any concerns they have. You may be able to find some children's books written specifically for stepfamilies.

- Be sure to take siblings out for special time at least monthly, if not weekly. Get them away from all the baby gear at home. Go on a walk, take them to the park or a movie, or go check out a music or retail store and giggle together in the aisles. Both biological and stepparents can do this, individually or together.

- Invite their age-appropriate help in getting baby used to the family. Maybe they can help pick out colors for the baby's room, choose clothes for baby, be part of your baby shower, or help with baby once they're here: Let them put on baby's socks, bottle feed, read baby stories, or entertain baby during bath time. With love, time, and support, half-siblings can have deep relationships like biological siblings.

- When possible, drop the "half" or "step" to better honor all relationships. Celebrate each child as a big brother or sister. For littler kids, you can give them a "big sister/brother" present when baby comes, like a stuffed animal, shirt, or jewelry. For older kids, be sure to note often how baby responds to them. Does baby watch them everywhere they go and get excited when they come home?

Older kids and teens will experience a new baby differently. They might feel the baby is different enough from them in age not to be competition. They might also be old enough to have their own lives outside that of their parents and may not fret as much about losing their parents' attention. They may take more or less interest in the new addition, depending on personality. Some teenagers have expressed to me frustration with their parents for having another child when their other children are already so much older. The best way to find out how your children feel about the situation is to ask them. Engaging your biological children with your new addition might be easier. As a stepparent, keep your focus on including them and inviting them to participate with the baby, but don't make doing so a requirement. If you, as a couple, have your older children babysit the new baby as this child moves into toddlerhood, be sure to treat them like a babysitter. Pay them, whenever possible, and outwardly appreciate their involvement and willingness to help.

There are certain circumstances to bringing home baby that you'll want to approach with added gentleness toward your children, such as when your child's other parent is absent or has died. Seeing the tenderness of their parent and stepparent with this new baby can bring up old feelings they don't always understand how to communicate. Was my other parent like that with me? Why did they have to go away? Approach these feelings in the way on which we focused in the "Expect Emotions" section in chapter 1 (see pages 10–14). Other circumstances may apply to most children, like their fears around whether you'll love baby more or confusion as to why baby gets to be with both parents all the time when they have to go between homes.

When appropriate, help kids see the positive side of separated or divorced parents. My stepdaughter was always a big fan of knowing that, no matter the holiday, she would always get more presents than any kid whose parents were still together (partly from having five sets of grandparents!). As difficult as going between homes can be, children can also experience a break when the baby goes through colic or teething. Be sure to note how happy you are when they get to spend time with you, and how much their new little sibling looks forward to seeing them. Verbalizing that you're glad they get a break and can spend positive time with their other parent is also okay. You're working to foster healthy relationships with all of their family members, including ex-spouses.

A new baby has the potential to bring your entire family closer together. In some families, a new baby helps stepchildren see their stepparent as more of a parent figure. They can really love their new stepsibling and become close with the stepparent through a shared interest.

The primary goal with integrating a new baby into your family system is to make the message to your other children clear: Love does not divide, it multiplies. Adding more people to your family simply means everybody has more love in their heart. Love isn't like a cake, with only a certain number of pieces to give out. Love stretches and grows to incorporate everyone you care about. This means showing the children that you still see and consider them, are curious about their experiences and feelings, and want to spend time with them. Even when you feel like you don't have any time and can barely see straight in those first few months of a new baby's life, there are always little moments you can sneak in with kids that will mean the world to them: an extra book, an invitation to snuggle on the couch, or an afternoon date of their choosing. These times may not happen as naturally in blended families as they can in first-time families, but with your continued effort and love, a new baby can bring you closer together.

Adult Children (and Their Families)

Some marriages happen later in life, when some or all children are already grown, sometimes with children of their own. If your children are adults, you might be wondering whether you'll really need to put in much work to blend your families. That your adult children will understand the importance of this new relationship and accept it intrinsically is easy to assume, especially if this later marriage is what you'd been longing for. After all, they're adults with their own lives, and you're no longer responsible for them.

When my mother and stepfather married, they briefly considered talking to someone to learn how to blend their families. They ultimately chose not to, thinking everyone was grown or nearly grown and would be able to figure things out. After all, they were so happy together. Shouldn't that happiness just trickle down? In speaking with my mother now, more than 10 years into their marriage, they wish they had sought help. There were bumps along the road that could have been smoothed out sooner had we known we would need to smooth them.

Since we didn't seek help, the family never fully became blended, and instead we have two somewhat separate families who share married parents. As adults we all get along, and I work to have my daughter know her full family, but the blended family will never be fully integrated.

Whether your children are little, teenagers, grown, or have children of their own, your intention and care in bringing families together matters. I often hear stories in my practice related to later marriages and the struggles around feeling involved in adult children's lives, especially with stepchildren or biological children who don't get along with your partner.

When parents remarry, it almost doesn't matter how old you are. Feeling like a child in an emotional situation with your parents, no matter your age, is both common and normal. This is because of two things. The first is the way your brain learned about the relationship with them. You were helpless and they taught you the way of the world. This is not something the brain easily forgets. The second is the power differential inherent in healthy parent-child relationships (and sometimes even in unhealthy ones), with children forever craving that parental nurturing and desire to feel safe in their parents' presence. This is why when you're hurt or scared, like during childbirth or divorce, you want them with you.

Imagine, then, you are 35 when your parents divorce. *Do you still feel 35?* You might temporarily feel younger, thrown back to a time in childhood when you worried about your parents or felt particularly comfortable with their relationship. Though adult children should be better able than younger children to navigate the emotional complexities of divorce, the split can still be sad, shocking, or confusing for them. So, when their parents remarry, they may not be ready to accept a new parent into their lives, and they may feel that they're beyond taking on more siblings. Since the relationships are not a required part of their daily life,

THE *DOS* AND *DON'TS* OF INTEGRATING ADULT CHILDREN

The key points in helping adult children blend into your family are functionally the same as with young children.

DO: Talk to them. Keep them involved and let them know about the importance of your relationship and hope for their support.

DON'T: Let them tell you what's best. Although dynamics change as they grow up, you can still make your expectations known, like everyone showing respect.

DO: Listen to their concerns. Hear them out and reassure them that you're making the best decision for you. Sometimes they just need to hear you're happy.

DON'T: Forget to let them know the benefits of the new relationship, like more people to love their kids.

DO: Spend time alone with your adult children, without your partner present. There will still be times your children just want their parent, even as adults.

DON'T: Leave out new stepsiblings. Encourage all adult children to engage one another in positive and fun ways.

bridging those gaps and building relationships takes more effort than when they're children.

Blending families is an active work in progress regardless of the age of your family. With effort, respect, and time, relationships with adult stepchildren and grandchildren can flourish and be enjoyable for everyone. Consider the ways your life is enhanced by blending families with adult children. Perhaps your children can have a stepsibling when they were never able to have a biological one. Maybe there are more opportunities for cousins for your grandchildren. Or perhaps you're given the opportunity to have children in your life if you never had your own. Look for the positive experiences to better appreciate them.

"Love does not divide, it multiplies. Adding more people to your family simply means everybody has more love in their heart."

CHAPTER FIVE
A New Future Together

Your work doesn't end once your family has come together. Blending a family can be challenging but also be deeply rewarding. One of the blessings is an opportunity to continue working together, learning from one another, and accepting each family member for their individuality. Though all relationships benefit from this consistent care, blended relationships require it for health and long-term success. The continuous effort encourages you to be present with your family and acknowledge the phases you go through together. This means looking at your partner, children, and stepchildren with fresh eyes each day. Though you may have known them for decades, all are continuously growing and changing. When you're intentional and resist falling into the trap of assuming who people are and how they will act or think today, you take yourself off autopilot and are better able to engage in your relationships in a meaningful way. This includes navigating routines and family cultures to create something that is distinctively yours. Your family will come with its own sets of holidays, celebrations, and routines. Maintain these and be open to creating new ones together. Breaking off into smaller family units at times is okay, so long as you still prioritize your entire family as a unit. Endeavor to check your assumptions at the door and embrace your family as they are, and you will set the stage for a connected, beautiful, and bright future together.

Rituals

As you come together, you may be faced with the challenge of blending your family cultures and traditions. You've had some conversations as a couple to help define this, but you'll also want to look at new family traditions you can create together. Think about what made your childhood special and work to offer that to your kids. You can also consider traditions your children grew used to in your first-time family and incorporate some of those comforting traditions. This can help the kids feel like they're allowed to still appreciate their old way of doing things when you introduce new ones. Rituals don't need to be extravagant, expensive endeavors. They can be simple and meaningful.

HOLIDAYS

Celebrating important holidays is a big part of many people's childhoods. As you think about honoring old traditions and creating new ones, sit down as a family and talk about which holidays are everyone's favorites and why. Maybe the kids love Christmas, one parent loves Thanksgiving, and the other Independence Day. But why? Maybe it's the presents, the turkey, or the fireworks. Or perhaps it's a special tradition, like a fondue dinner, saying what you're thankful for, or those great backyard barbecues. Make no assumptions when you're discussing holidays. Instead, delve deeper into why your family members love those moments. Do they have a favorite type of firework? Which part of the dinner do they like best?

Smaller holidays can mean the world to a blended family, including Mother's Day and Father's Day. Be sure to encourage your kids and extended family to acknowledge the stepparents in your family in addition to biological parents. Stepparents still guide, care for, and work tirelessly for the kids in their lives. I was so appreciative when my stepdaughter's mom helped her create a Mother's Day present for me. This tends to be easier for families who have experience with blending, as families who don't may not think to extend wishes. You can help support positive connections and strong relationships in families blending together by acknowledging the role each person plays.

Be sure to respect everyone's feelings with celebrating. Pay special attention to and be conscientious about how the children are feeling about the changes. They often have spent their entire lives with holidays and celebrations being a certain way, and may mourn the loss of what used to be. Take a stance of openness in order to create space for them to go through this process. Seek to understand their experiences and look for opportunities to help adjust them slowly, integrate pieces of what matters to them, or carve out time to keep those traditions alive. Keeping traditions that were around before this new family can help ease the transition. For example, did the family exchange presents, attend a ceremony or service, and invite extended family to participate? Quite possibly, your families celebrated things differently. Talk through your normal holiday routines and see if there's a way to incorporate both into your new traditions.

If the other biological parent has the kids for some holidays, try to include the kids in your celebrations as much as possible. They won't be able to be part of all the family traditions on both sides, and that can be tricky for them. They may end up feeling like they're ultimately missing out regardless of where they go, so find little ways to weave them into your holidays. In my family, we've found that my stepdaughter will never be able to celebrate Christmas with my side of the family. On years we have her, we go to my husband's family's celebrations, and the years we're with my family, she's with her mom. I certainly feel disappointed that I don't get to share the holiday with my family with her, but my job is to respect her family on both sides and not push the issue of having her join. Instead, we find ways to take her with us to celebrate in the days surrounding the holidays so she knows she's part of my family, too.

With more family members come more split holidays. Some families coordinate all those involved and rotate on a strict schedule, whereas others may go with the flow or resort to fighting over who gets the family when. If you can feel confident and united as a family, then you can communicate your wishes to your extended family.

Trust that as time goes on, you'll learn what works best for you. Holidays can be stressful no matter how well you've coordinated everything, so be sure to remain flexible in your mind, open in your heart, and grateful for any time you can spend together. Communicate how much you love your kids and want them to be able to enjoy time with all their family. Keep your focus on the upside of splitting the holidays when you can, but keep the lines of communication open for them to talk about their feelings. Maybe they're excited they get double the presents, or maybe they're sad they always miss someone on major holidays. See their feelings as understandable and acceptable, just as yours will be when you miss your kids. Fight off the stress of the holidays by collecting sweet moments of connection together. Try verbalizing your gratitude or appreciation for those moments to help the family remember them.

Here's one idea for a new tradition. For the month before a holiday special to your family, set a jar on your counter with a stack of little pieces of paper and a pen nearby. Throughout the month each family member writes down moments and things they are grateful for, folds up the paper, and puts them in the jar. On or near the holiday gathering, sit down and pass the jar around, reading aloud moments that the family has enjoyed. This helps you come together with gratitude and laughter before the holiday is in full swing. What other tradition could your family start?

BIRTHDAYS

They come once a year for each of us, so how can we enjoy them as a family? For the kids, will you do joint parties with the rest of their biological family, will they have two parties, or will they rotate which family they celebrate with each year? Are you big on celebrating birthdays, are they just another day for you, or do you abhor them? Everyone feels differently about their birthdays. Again, be curious about what each family member looks forward to or not. Honor the differences and be open to varied perspectives.

Share with your family your most memorable birthdays and what made them so amazing (or not!). Knowing birthday preferences for each of your family members not only brings you closer by understanding what's important to each person, but also helps you celebrate in a way that makes everyone feel special and loved.

If you don't like your own birthday, or birthdays become stressful because of custody issues, try to lessen their impact by remaining flexible. Perhaps the best birthday celebration is simply to let your loved one know you care with a hand-made card, a special dinner, or breakfast in bed. No matter how messy custody issues get, with your kids' birthdays, those issues take a backseat. The key to loving others is to wish them happiness, so whether you get to spend the day with your children or not, hope for a happy day. The same goes for when you don't like birthdays, but your partner does. Think of the birthday as a time to celebrate and appreciate the person in your life, regardless of whether you want the same kind of attention around your day.

"You're building a family, and you're also building a team."

MILESTONE CELEBRATIONS

Wedding bells, a graduation procession, baby shower, or anniversary celebration are all times when families come together to celebrate and support one another. What are some milestones your family has already reached and how have you managed them? What lessons did you learn from those experiences that will help you in the future?

Whether your family comes together to celebrate or does so separately may depend on the relationships you're able to build with your ex-spouse. If you've navigated the tricky waters of separation and have found a healthy co-parenting relationship, milestones will be easier to manage. You may still find yourself in sometimes awkward situations at one another's homes for celebrations for graduation or engagement parties down the road, but you've already laid a foundation of respect and cooperation. If you feel willing and able, save seats for one another at recitals or big games. Show up if invited to celebrate your ex-spouse's new children, as doing this can encourage your children's relationship with their stepsiblings. Know your limits, be willing to stretch them slightly, but also be honest with yourself. If you're deeply uncomfortable, you won't show up as your best self.

If you're engaging in parallel parenting, you may struggle to find a balance in who attends which events. Perhaps both of you are able to go to their recitals and big games, but you sit separately to avoid any potential conflict. When you greet your kid afterward, focus on them instead of avoiding or confronting your ex. Celebrate your child and then be sure to allow them space to celebrate with their other parent. Keep an air of respect and poise at these events and resist any temptation to engage negatively with your ex (or your partner's ex). Your children will feel the pressure if you're only willing to show up when their other parent won't be there. There's no good reason to put them through that. Try to show up if being there is safe to do and be unfazed by the rest. Nothing anyone says can hurt your feelings or upset you without your permission. If you feel baited at a shared event, remember you are there for your child. *Your children will respect you more if you can notice the bait, but not take it.*

In the event your children have lost their other parent or have an absent parent, you may want to take special consideration regarding who comes to their big moments. Depending on the relationship they have with your new partner, your new partner may be able to step into the role of parent, temporarily, to show up for your kids. This might be a parent-child dance, a school overnight trip, or coaching a soccer or baseball team. As a stepparent, you won't ever try to take the place of their missing parent, but you may be able to fill some of the space.

Continue Building Your Relationships

As the dust settles on the initial blending, you can relax and look forward to the future with your new family. Your family will find its rhythm, and when this is in place, you will find yours. Seeing a light at the end of the tunnel when you're first beginning to blend a family can be hard. With effort and consistency, though, you have the power to create a strong, connected family. Keep future outcomes in mind if you're feeling discouraged and know time will make things easier.

TIPS FOR WHOM TO INVITE TO MILESTONES AND CELEBRATIONS

- Ask the kids whom they wish to have as part of the celebration. They may surprise you with whom they would and would not like to have join the party that day.

- Offer olive branches by inviting exes to celebrations. If they decline, try not to take it personally. You're each navigating your own comfort levels and want to be respectful.

- Incorporate all sides, if possible, when celebrating milestones and birthdays for the children. If your comfort allows, invite exes to family celebrations, as well.

- Remember whom this is all for: your children. Show your children they can enjoy life's great moments without anxiety about whom to invite or how their parents will act.

- If your child has lost their other parent, be open to having symbolic representations of this parent in big moments throughout your child's life. Honoring them can ease the pain.

YOUR PARTNER

You've learned about the importance of your relationship with your partner as the foundation for your new family. Learning to communicate in a more productive way will serve you well as time goes on. When you both work to talk through any issues that come up, problem-solving and making decisions will get easier. If your attempts at communication in the beginning are a little clunky, don't give up hope. Your first attempts at sitting up when you were a baby were pretty clumsy, too, and yet you're able to sit up on your own now. You may have taken a few spills or fallen on your face, but each time you tried again, your muscles strengthened and adjusted for the next attempt. Emotional experiences require the same muscle development. If you're new to a skill, training your body, mind, and heart to do the skill properly will take time. Then one day you'll find success—you'll be able to have an effective conversation together that leaves you both feeling understood and connected. You may still have a hard time talking about difficult topics, but your communication skills will keep getting stronger. Eventually it may feel as though you've always been able to engage in positive, empathetic, supportive dialogue with your partner.

As your communication improves, your connection will as well. With your intention to greet your partner each day and be curious about them, you nurture your relationship. When obstacles present themselves, look at them as opportunities to grow. With every step you take to solve a problem and bring your family together, you're growing closer and strengthening your bond. The more bumps in the road, the more skilled you become at working together. Because of this, your relationship has enormous potential to be fulfilling, supportive, and deeply satisfying.

Look to each other for support and be intentional about seeing your partner as your ally.

The same principles apply to your parenting. At first, you may feel like you must overcome a huge obstacle because your parenting situation is more complex. But this complexity also means you have more opportunities to learn and grow as a parent. With every misstep, you learn to take accountability, apologize, and improve your approach for the next time. You'll need to work together to meld into a solid parenting unit. As time goes on, you'll learn more from each other, build upon your strengths, and lean on each other to soften the edges. Your relationship, including your communication and parenting, offers you an amazing opportunity to strengthen your bond.

Keeping your relationship strong will take effort, too, but the payoff will be that you weather the difficult times better. Healthy and connected relationships create resilience or a buffer to protect you from bumps in the road down the line—like a positive snowball. Just as negative things can build if you don't give them time and attention, so can positive experiences when you give them the care and intention they need. The more you communicate, work together, and lean on your partner for emotional support, the easier that becomes and the more rewards you'll get. If having those conversations feels good, you'll be more likely to engage in them again. Keep building your relationship in this way and focus on seeing the positive aspects of your partner and family.

YOUR CHILDREN

How will your children benefit from being part of your blended family in the long run? This is a meaningful question to ask yourself as you set your sights on having a happy, healthy blended family. Maybe they'll get siblings they never had before or a chance for a positive relationship with another parent if their other biological parent is absent. Maybe you're feeling uncertain about how this will benefit them, and you need a little nudge in a positive direction.

One crucial step you can take is to focus on modeling for children how you hope they'll grow up. If your previous relationship was not your ideal model of the type of relationship you hope your children will find someday, how can you create that in your new partnership? Perhaps through your new relationship your children will see what a healthy relationship is and what connection and love feel like. Maybe they'll have a better chance at experiencing an affectionate, playful, and close family within your new blended one. This new family is an opportunity to give your children what all children deserve: happy, healthy, and emotionally attuned caregivers. Your children get to see the happy version of you, and thus experience you at your personal best.

By engaging in this new family, your children will also have the opportunity to learn important lessons. They'll learn how to problem solve in complex relationships and living arrangements. They'll have opportunities to practice advocating for what they need, identifying and sharing their emotional experience, and developing responsibility for how they engage in relationships. They'll learn how to communicate with others in more productive and respectful ways. Children of blended families are given the good fortune of seeing that the world is bigger than they are, and that the concept of family is malleable.

You can support your children in learning these valuable lessons as they navigate the changing waters of their new family. By setting and practicing each day open communication as a family, you can help your kids learn how to navigate through these experiences. At different times your children will need empathy, an alternative viewpoint, or a challenge when they're stuck. By nurturing the relationship you have with your children, you can also help them see the good in their blended family. Your children, whether small or grown, want to know that they are loved and seen for who they are. If you're able to greet them as they are and express an unconditional love and positive regard for them, you're giving your children one of the greatest gifts a parent can give.

Your relationship with and your love for your children can also keep you afloat on hard days. If you're feeling overwhelmed or uncertain, returning to this love can help you relax and come into the present moment. You can lean on your love for them without them ever knowing, simply by stopping the chatter in your mind and noticing how beautifully they are growing up. Looking for the amazing parts of your children helps you create and maintain deeper bonds with them as they grow.

YOUR STEPCHILDREN

The possibility of stepparents having great relationships with their stepchildren is there. If your relationship is great right out of the gate, keep the positive experiences going by expressing gratitude to your kids. Do what you can to maintain what's working and continually look for opportunities to add to the great mix you have. Look at special dates or traditions you have with your stepchildren, and figure out ways to celebrate and appreciate each other one on one. If you have a good relationship with their other biological parent, how can you keep the energy positive between you? Like all relationships, a positive connection with your stepchildren requires acknowledging what is going well, continually putting in effort and care to keep things from going stale, and apologizing when you make eventual missteps.

One great way to acknowledge and work together through those awkward or tense moments with one another as you're building your relationship is to speak them aloud. Agree on what you and your stepkids can hear to help you displace tension before it builds. You can say, "Whoops! I stepped in it a bit there, didn't I?" or, "Uh-oh, I must have touched on a sensitive area."

If your relationship with your stepchildren started off on the wrong foot, a change is not too late. Even if you've had years of difficult interactions, there are steps you can take to make improvements. I've seen positive changes with families who have struggled for most of their young children's lives, as well as with grown children after a decade of problematic interactions. Your goal, if this is where you find yourself, is to examine where things went awry. Most likely, everyone in the child's life has played a role in getting the relationship to this place, including you.

There's no shame in acknowledging where you've participated in making a difficult relationship. Maybe you came on too intensely, as I did in my relationship with my stepdaughter, and you need to learn to take a backseat to their biological parent. Maybe you haven't been involved enough or you've struggled to get along with their other biological parent. Acknowledging your role in the way the relationship has developed is the first step to finding a solution.

Expect that the process of unlearning the negative patterns in which you've been stuck and relearning new ones takes time. Lots of time. This process also takes patience, forgiveness for yourself and others, and repetition of the new way. How many years have you been engaging in a manner that doesn't work well for your family? How long, then, might it take for your family to find a new path? Eventually old paths get overgrown and new paths are worn. Your commitment to consistency will light your way. Look for little improvements—like your children asking for help with homework—and celebrate them.

How you feel about your stepchild, their other biological parent, and your partner impacts your relationship with the children. Children are astute at recognizing emotional experiences and, with or without their knowledge, reflecting these to us through their behavior. If you're frustrated, your stepchildren are more likely to act in a frustrating way—not only because you're looking for them to be frustrating, but because they can sense what you're feeling and don't have a better way to express their own feelings. Nothing turns a fussy kid around faster than a calm caregiver.

Regardless of where you are today with your stepchildren, keep your messages to your children and stepchildren positive and supportive. Build upon the foundation you've already laid and keep your eye on the great aspects of them. Try statements like the following to help focus your mind on encouraging them, thus continually improving your connection with them:

- You are so brave.

- I am proud of you.

- You worked really hard on that.

- You amaze me.

- I appreciate how helpful you are.

- I always enjoy spending time with you.

IF YOU NEED HELP

Blending families isn't easy. You might find parts, or all, of your family are in need of additional support. Find a community that can rally around your family. You can seek out other blended families for camaraderie. As stepparents, find other stepparents in whom you can confide. When possible, try not to blend on an island. Build some bridges and create a tribe that can hear your challenges and help you see the beauty in what you're trying to accomplish.

There are also skilled professionals who can help you and your family along the way. You can reach out to a licensed professional counselor or a marriage and family therapist for individual, family, group, and couples counseling.

Think about what you're hoping to accomplish and have some questions ready as you interview possible helpers. Do they have experience in helping blended families? What is their outlook on what success looks like in blended families? Does this outlook match yours? Keep your eye out for someone who feels like a good fit. Meeting a few people before deciding who is best for your family is absolutely okay.

If you're in a deeper crisis, there are some in-home programs that support parenting in real-time. Reach out to your local community mental health center for resources. If you're looking for group counseling, your children's school can also be a resource. Also, local governments can have lists of support systems for their communities. The right help is out there.

Find Time for Family Fun

We've come to the end of our journey together, but yours is just beginning. You have the skills, and you're building on your communication and connection. Once you feel like you're getting some footing, this is the last essential piece: *Have fun*.

One of the best ways to build connection as a family is to get out there and enjoy one another. You're working hard at making your family feel cohesive, and you also need to sit back, relax, and enjoy the fruits of your labor. Laughter is good for mental, emotional, and physical well-being. Laughing together can bring you closer, create shared meaning, and bring your collective blood pressure down. It also triggers the brain to release endorphins and oxytocin, a chemical responsible for creating bonds between people. Research has found that laughter is an important piece in forming social bonds.

Celebrate getting to be part of one another's lives and give a high five when you navigate a tricky situation with grace. As your connections improve and you gain insight into one another's foibles, you can start to laugh things off when they go awry. If you have positive relationships, you can catch yourself and one another in moments that could go sideways, and use humor to relieve some of the tension.

Sometimes you may have fun all together as this new family, whereas at others you'll have time with the original, separate families. As much as your family can benefit from time all together to relax and enjoy, children will benefit from some alone time with their biological parents as well. This time, especially when they are doing activities that are special to that relationship, can help them feel more open and flexible with incorporating stepfamily into their lives. Look at these moments as special for each child and encourage those positive relationships.

You're building a family, and you're also building a team. This team will be with you for the rest of your life. Your team will be there to cheer one another on, support one another in sadness or grief, and remind one another to relax and have fun. You are making a team that supports all of you and understands that each of you has different interests and needs. This team is about trusting and caring for one another, sticking together even when times get rough, and knowing that no matter what, you are not alone.

Here are 10 great ways to have fun and celebrate with your family:

1. Go on a hike or walk that everyone can enjoy.

2. Go camping together, even if in the backyard. Read stories, make shadow puppets.

3. Blast some music and have impromptu dance parties.

4. Create tradition by cooking a meal of the children's choice with them.

5. Get out paints and pick some rocks from the yard to make rock pets together.

6. Take them to live music or their favorite band's concert.

7. Share an ice cream treat.

8. Play video games that require you to work together to win.

9. Go shopping together to try on funny hats and glasses that make you laugh.

10. Find moments to let them know just how much you love having them around.

That's it. You're ready. Go have some fun and remember to enjoy the adventure you're on with your new blended family.

RESOURCES

Brown, Brené. *Daring Greatly: How the Courage to Be Vulnerable Transforms the Way We Live, Love, Parent, and Lead.* New York: Avery Press, 2015.

"Discipline that Works." Aha! Parenting.com. Accessed August 2019. https://www.ahaparenting.com/parenting-tools/Discipline.

Gottman, John M., and Nan Silver. *The Seven Principles for Making Marriage Work: A Practical Guide from the Country's Foremost Relationship Expert.* New York: Harmony Press, 2015.

Johnson, Kimberly Ann. *The Fourth Trimester: A Postpartum Guide to Healing Your Body, Balancing Your Emotions, and Restoring Your Vitality.* Boulder, CO: Shambhala, 2017.

Markham, Laura. *Peaceful Parent, Happy Kids: How to Stop Yelling and Start Connecting.* New York: Perigee, 2012.

"Our Mission" The Gottman Institute. Accessed July 30, 2019. https://www.gottman.com/about/.

Papernow, Patricia L. *Surviving and Thriving in Stepfamily Relationships: What Works and What Doesn't.* New York and East Sussex, UK: Routledge, 2013.

Sapolsky, Robert M. *Why Zebras Don't Get Ulcers: The Acclaimed Guide to Stress, Stress-Related Diseases, and Coping.* 3rd ed. New York: Henry Holt, 2004.

Siegel, Daniel J., and Tina Payne Bryson. *No-Drama Discipline: The Whole-Brain Way to Calm the Chaos and Nurture Your Child's Developing Mind.* New York: Bantam Books, 2016.

Soule, Amanda Blake. *The Creative Family Manifesto: Encouraging Imagination and Nurturing Family Connections*. Boulder, CO: Roost Books, 2017.

Vannoy, Steven W. *The 10 Greatest Gifts I Give My Children: Parenting from the Heart*. New York: Touchstone, 2014.

Wisdom, Susan, and Jennifer Green. *Stepcoupling: Creating and Sustaining a Strong Marriage in Today's Blended Family*. New York: Three Rivers Press, 2002.

REFERENCES

Altenhofen, Shannon, Robert Clyman, Christina Little, Megan Baker, and Zeynep Biringen. "Attachment Security in Three-Year-Olds Who Entered Substitute Care in Infancy." *Infant Mental Health Journal* 34, no. 5 (2013): 435–45. doi:10.1002/imhj.21401.

Assor, Avi, Guy Roth, and Edward L. Deci. "The Emotional Costs of Parents' Conditional Regard: A Self-Determination Theory Analysis." *Journal of Personality* 72, no. 1 (Feb. 2004): 47–88.

Bratton, Sue C., Gary L. Landreth, Theresa Kellam, Sandra R. Blackard. *Child Parent Relationship Therapy (CPRT) Treatment Manual: A 10-Session Filial Therapy Model for Training Parents*. New York: Routledge/Taylor & Francis Group, 2006.

Chapman, Gary D. *The 5 Love Languages: The Secret to Love That Lasts.* Chicago: Northfield, 2015.

Glass, George S., and David, Tabatsky. *Blending Families Successfully: Helping Parents and Kids Navigate the Challenges So That Everyone Ends Up Happy*. New York: Skyhorse, 2014.

Gottman, John M., James Coan, Sybil Carrere, and Catherine Swanson. "Predicting Marital Happiness and Stability from Newlywed Interactions." *Journal of Marriage and Family* 60, no. 1 (Feb. 1998): 5–22. doi:10.2307/353438.

Harman, Jennifer J., Edward Kruk, and Denise A. Hines. "Parental Alienating Behaviors: An Unacknowledged Form of Family Violence." *Psychological Bulletin* 144, no. 12 (2018): 1275–299. doi:10.1037/bul0000175.

Jacobson, Tamar. *Everyone Needs Attention: Helping Young Children Thrive.* St. Paul, MN: Redleaf, 2018.

Johnston, Janet, Vivienne Roseby, and Kathryn Kuehnle. *In the Name of the Child: A Developmental Approach to Understanding and Helping Children of Conflicted and Violent Divorce.* 2nd ed. New York: Springer, 2009.

King, Valarie, Lisa M. Boyd, and Maggie L. Thorsen. "Adolescents' Perceptions of Family Belonging in Stepfamilies." *Journal of Marriage and Family* 77, no. 3 (2015): 761–74. doi:10.1111/jomf.12181.

Manninen, Sandra, Lauri Tuominen, Robin I. Dunbar, Tomi Karjalainen, Jussi Hirvonen, Eveliina Arponen, Riitta Hari, Iiro P. Jääskeläinen, Mikko Sams, and Lauri Nummenmaa. "Social Laughter Triggers Endogenous Opioid Release in Humans." *The Journal of Neuroscience* 37, no. 25 (2017): 6125–131. doi:10.1523/jneurosci.0688-16.2017.

"New Co-parenting Communication Tool: The Vault: Our Newest Mobile App Feature." Talking Parents. Accessed July 30, 2019. https://talkingparents.com/home.

Papernow, Patricia L. "The Stepfamily Cycle: An Experiential Model of Stepfamily Development." *Family Relations* 33, no. 3 (Jul. 1984): 355–63. doi:10.2307/584706.

Rees, Corinne. "Childhood attachment." *British Journal of General Practice* 57, no. 544 (2007): 920–22. Accessed July 15, 2019. doi:10.3399/096016407782317955.

Visher, Emily B., and John S. Visher. "Common Problems of Stepparents and Their Spouses." *American Journal of Orthopsychiatry* 48, no. 2 (April 1978): 252–62. doi:10.1111/j.1939-0025.1978.tb01313.x.

Wurtele, Sandy K., and Feather Berkower. *Off Limits: A Parents' Guide to Keeping Kids Safe from Sexual Abuse.* Brandon, VT: Safer Society Press, 2010.

INDEX

ACKNOWLEDGMENTS

The opportunity to write this book has been a gift and an honor. This book would not be possible without the love and support of my husband, who walks this journey with me. I owe a thank you to my four parents for showing me the love a blended family can bring, and to my siblings (full, half, and step) for working toward creating our own versions of family. Thank you to my tribe of women who have helped see me through. And thank you to my daughter and stepdaughter, for understanding my sacred nap-time writing windows and showing me the way.

The love my family and friends bring lights up my life.

I owe a debt of gratitude to Callisto Media for trusting in me to bring together this book for families, and to my editor, Eliza Kirby, for supporting me through the process and polishing this manuscript with grace.

ABOUT THE AUTHOR

With over a decade of experience, **Danielle Schlagel** is a licensed professional counselor, licensed addictions counselor, registered play therapist-supervisor, and the owner of a mental health practice: seity.org. She has worked with families from around the world, including blended families of all shapes and sizes. She provides consultations with and supervises other professionals working with children and families, and completes child and family investigations for custody issues through the courts. Danielle writes with warmth and honesty and firmly believes in practicing what she preaches. She and her husband blend their family together in Boulder, Colorado.

CPSIA information can be obtained
at www.ICGtesting.com
Printed in the USA
LVHW022127211019
634864LV00003B/3/P